WELL-BEING

Productivity and Happiness at Work

Ivan Robertson

Director, Robertson Cooper
Professor of Organizational Psychology, Leeds University Business School

and

Cary Cooper

Distinguished Professor of Organizational Psychology and Health, Lancaster University
Director, Robertson Cooper Ltd

palgrave
macmillan

First published 2011 by
PALGRAVE MACMILLAN

Palgrave Macmillan in the UK is an imprint of Macmillan Publishers Limited,
registered in England, company number 785998, of Houndmills, Basingstoke,
Hampshire RG21 6XS.

Palgrave Macmillan in the US is a division of St Martin's Press LLC,
175 Fifth Avenue, New York, NY 10010.

Palgrave Macmillan is the global academic imprint of the above companies
and has companies and representatives throughout the world.

Palgrave® and Macmillan® are registered trademarks in the United States,
the United Kingdom, Europe and other countries.

ISBN 978–0–230–24995–0

This book is printed on paper suitable for recycling and made from fully
managed and sustained forest sources. Logging, pulping and manufacturing
processes are expected to conform to the environmental regulations of the
country of origin.

A catalogue record for this book is available from the British Library.

A catalog record for this book is available from the Library of Congress.

10   9   8   7   6   5   4   3   2   1
20   19   18   17   16   15   14   13   12   11

Printed and bound in Great Britain by
CPI Antony Rowe, Chippenham and Eastbourne

There can be no health without mental health

United Nations Secretary-General Ban Ki-moon:
Message on World Mental Health Day,
10 October 2010

CONTENTS

CONTENTS

LIST OF FIGURES, TABLES AND BOXES

Figures

Tables

Boxes

FOREWORD

This book is about well-being, productivity and happiness at work, and about ways to preserve and promote such phenomena. It is also remarkably timely.

Not long ago, French President Nicholas Sarkozy established a distinguished commission to report on ways to measure the well-being of an entire population. In 2008, the British government received a major report, prepared by an equally distinguished commission, on "Mental Capital and Well-being", including many proposals for political implementation. And even more recently, Great Britain's present Prime Minister David Cameron commissioned his country's official statistics Agency to prepare an index intended to measure national well-being, as a complement to current measurements of its Gross National Product (GNP).

In spite of these recent references, the basic idea about well-being and quality of life as political goals is not new. According to Greek physician Galen, employment is "nature's physician, essential to human happiness". Although according to John Stuart Mills "it is possible to do without happiness. It is done involuntarily by nineteen-twentieths of mankind", William James maintained that "how to gain, how to keep, how to recover happiness is in fact for most men at all times the secret motive of all they do, and of all they are willing to endure".

A prerequisite for all this is that people, indeed, have a job, and that this job is of reasonably good quality. This is nicely summarized in the European Union's Lisbon strategy "More and Better Jobs". Unfortunately, countless European workers remain unemployed or have jobs that are patho- rather than salutogenic.

This book deals with essential aspects of all these issues.

Its first part is concerned with why well-being matters. It tells the story of the benefits for individuals of well-being in the workplace and goes on with an analysis of demonstrable benefits also for organizations, including lower sickness-absence, better retention of talented people and more satisfied customers/users/patients. It further discusses how well-being is related to employee engagement.

Part 2 is devoted to what is meant by well-being, as it includes both positive emotions and a sense of purpose in life, also explaining how it could and should be measured.

Part 3 has its focus on the determinants of well-being, within as well as outside working life.

Part 4 aims at the benefits of well-being, with building personal resilience as well as healthy workplaces as two major objectives.

Part 5 presents nine important chapters with highly illustrative and relevant case studies, from both public and private sector workplaces and both from the US and a number of EU Member States including Great Britain.

All this is presented and discussed in considerable depth by the eminent scientists in the chapters of this important new volume. It is an essential resource for scholars, researchers and practitioners in occupational health who aim to make workplaces healthier, happier and more productive for all concerned. It is also an important resource for managers and labor unionists and in general for all those in public and occupational health who are concerned with health and productivity issues in workplaces.

Lennart Levi, MD, PhD
Emeritus Professor of Psychosocial Medicine (Karolinska Institutet)
Member of the Swedish Parliament (2006–2010)
Stockholm, January 2011

ACKNOWLEDGMENTS

We hope that this book will be useful and that it will convince many people of the benefits of positive psychological well-being in organizations. We also hope that it will stimulate those with responsibility in organizations to take action.

The book could not have been produced without the help of many people. First and foremost, our grateful thanks go to the authors of the case study chapters for the time, effort and skill that they have put in. We also thank the host organizations for the case studies for allowing the reports of work carried out to be published in this book.

Our colleagues at Robertson Cooper Ltd and the universities of Leeds and Lancaster also deserve our thanks for providing the supportive, stimulating and challenging working environment that enabled us to produce the book. Several colleagues have contributed to the case study chapters and their names are acknowledged in those chapters. Laura Heathcock deserves special mention for ploughing through early drafts of the manuscript and providing insightful comments and suggestions. Of course, as ever, the first prizes for support, encouragement and patience go to Kathy Robertson and Rachel Cooper!

At Palgrave Macmillan we are particularly grateful to Stephen Rutt for recognizing that this is a book on a timely and important topic and for the patience and support of Eleanor Davey Corrigan who shepherded the book through all its stages of production with patience and skill.

PART 1

WHY WELL-BEING MATTERS

CHAPTER 1

FOR INDIVIDUALS

Work can make you sick – and work can make you happy. Which one happens depends on who you are, what you do and how you are treated at work. Work that is rewarding, involving good relationships with colleagues and opportunities to feel a sense of achievement on a regular basis is a key factor in psychological well-being (PWB). Good PWB, as we shall see later in this chapter, is linked to good physical heath. Dull and monotonous work, difficult relationships with others and work that is impossibly demanding 'or lacks meaning' damages resilience, PWB and physical health. Later chapters will explain how PWB can be damaged or enhanced by work and will also cover the key workplace factors that influence PWB. This chapter sets the scene for what follows by explaining why PWB at work matters and how it is linked to overall sickness and health.

Overall, well-being includes three main parts: physical, social and psychological well-being (Figure 1.1). This book focuses on psychological (mental) well-being in particular. That does not mean that the other forms of well-being are less important than PWB.

In the workplace however, when industrial accidents and dangerous working conditions are set to one side, PWB is most important – and (apart from accidents, etc.) work has more direct impact on PWB, rather than the physical or social aspects of well-being.

At the most basic level, PWB is quite similar to other terms that refer to positive mental states, such as happiness or satisfaction, and in many ways it is not necessary, or helpful, in a book like this to worry about fine distinctions between such terms. If I say that I'm happy, or very satisfied with my life you can be pretty sure that my PWB is quite high! It is important though to explain that some other popular terms such as "job satisfaction" or "motivation" are not the same as PWB. Job satisfaction is about how satisfied someone feels with their current job; this is certainly a factor in PWB but, for example, it is

3

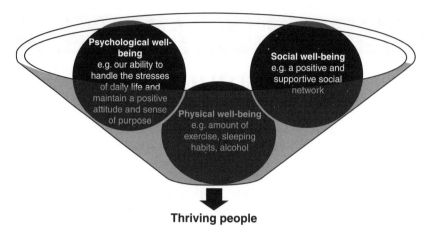

FIGURE 1.1   **The three components of well-being**

perfectly possible for someone to be satisfied with their specific job but be very unhappy about relationships with some colleagues, or the quality of management and supervision that they receive. The same goes for motivation. I could be very energized by a work task and work very hard at it because I feel it's important and I don't want to let people down, but the workload involved and lack of resources available could make me frustrated and unhappy. Although we will look more closely at the specific meaning of PWB later in this chapter, for the moment we can say that good PWB is more or less the same as being happy at work. Later in this chapter we will also look at the specific evidence showing how PWB at work has an impact on physical health, job performance and things such as career success. To place the role of work in context we begin by reviewing how PWB is associated with overall success in life, with physical illness and other related factors.

PWB IS LINKED TO SUCCESS AND HEALTH

Research studies have shown that higher levels of PWB are linked to higher levels of income, more successful marriages and friendships and better health and, as we shall see later, better work performance. Of course, talking of a link between PWB and success in life immediately raises an important question – which comes first? In other words, does success come before higher levels of PWB, bringing the (obvious) outcome of increased happiness, or might it be that higher levels of PWB actually lead to successful outcomes? In fact, it seems quite likely that both of these effects happen. It is self-evident that doing well at something that matters to us brings psychological benefits, including increased PWB but it does also seem to be the case that people who develop higher levels of PWB are better equipped to deal with life and are more likely to make a success of things. What is the evidence for this?

Some research on this topic involves looking at happiness scores for a group of people and also looking at how these people fare on the types of life factors that have been mentioned above – marriage, friendships, income and so on. In practice there are quite a lot of studies of this kind (referred to as "cross-sectional" studies) and they generally produce the same conclusion: that greater happiness is associated with better results on the life factors. For example, studies have shown that in three primary life domains (work, relationships and health) people higher on PWB come out better (Lyubomirsky et al., 2005). As well as these primary life domains the cross-sectional research also shows that PWB is linked to many other characteristics that are seen by our culture and society as desirable, such as positive views of self and others, popularity with other people, coping with distress and better immune system functioning.

Although this type of research shows overwhelming support for the link between PWB and life success, it cannot tell us for certain whether PWB leads to success or vice versa. Longitudinal studies are needed to answer this question properly. In longitudinal studies data on PWB are collected at one point in time and then at a later point data on the life factors are collected. These types of studies make it more possible to draw conclusions about cause and effect. Such studies are especially powerful if the effect of the starting position on the life factors is also taken into account. For example, if two groups who are similar in terms of immune system functioning at the beginning, but with different levels of PWB, are compared over time. Sonja Lyubomirsky and her colleagues, Laura King and Ed Diener, looked at all of the longitudinal studies that they could find. Broadly, although the evidence was less extensive, they found the same conclusions as the cross-sectional studies. They found that "Study after study shows that happiness precedes important outcomes and indicators of thriving, including fulfilling and productive work, satisfying relationships and superior mental and physical health and longevity" (Lyubomirsky et al., 2005, p. 834). More recent research has confirmed their findings. Yoichi Chida and Andrew Steptoe (2008) looked at 35 separate longitudinal studies examining the relationship between PWB and mortality. They found that positive PWB had a protective effect. Overall, the research that they examined showed that positive well-being was associated with reduced mortality rates for healthy people and reduced mortality for patients with specific illnesses, such as immune system viruses and kidney failure. They concluded that "... positive psychological well-being has a favourable effect on survival in both healthy and diseased populations" (Chida and Steptoe, 2008, p. 741).

Actually, PWB has two important facets. The first of these refers to the extent to which people experience positive emotions and feelings of happiness. Sometimes this aspect of PWB is referred to as subjective well-being (Diener, 2000). Subjective well-being is a necessary part of overall PWB but on its own it is not enough. To see why this is so, imagine being somewhere that you really enjoy, perhaps sitting on a yacht in the sunshine, with your favorite food and drink and some good company – or alone if that's how you'd prefer it! For most people that would be very enjoyable for a week or two but imagine doing it not just for a week but forever! There are very few people who would find that prospect enjoyable. The old saying may be true, you can have too much of a good thing. What this example brings home is that to really feel good we need to experience purpose and meaning, in addition to positive emotions. So, the two important ingredients in PWB are the subjective happy feelings brought on by something we enjoy AND the feeling that what we are doing with our lives has some meaning and purpose. The term "Hedonic" well-being is normally used to refer to the subjective feelings of happiness, and the less well-known term "Eudaimonic" well-being is used to refer to the purposeful aspect of PWB. Psychologist Carol Ryff has developed a very clear model that breaks down eudaimonic well-being into six key parts. Figure 1.2 illustrates both hedonic and eudaimonic PWB.

In further research Ryff and her colleagues (Ryff et al., 2004) have explored the links between both aspects of PWB and biological indicators of physical health. As with the other research described above they found many relationships between PWB and biological markers of health, such as levels of cortisol (the "stress" hormone), risk of heart problems, immune system functioning and sleep quality. Interestingly in their study they found that hedonic well-being showed relatively

Eudaimonic well-being terms
- ✓ Self-acceptance
- ✓ Environmental mastery
- ✓ Positive relationships
- ✓ Personal growth
- ✓ Purpose in life
- ✓ Autonomy

Hedonic well-being terms
- ✓ Happiness
- ✓ Subjective well-being
- ✓ Positive emotions

FIGURE 1.2   **Hedonic and eudaimonic aspects of PWB**

few links with the biological markers but eudaimonic PWB was more strongly associated with them. These results may have been influenced by the relatively small sample used in their work (135), or by the nature of the sample (women over 61 years of age).

Despite some reservations and the inevitable need for more research, the results of existing research point very strongly to links between PWB and life and health outcomes. So, if the beneficial effects of high PWB are established, a new question arises: how does PWB protect people against illness or lead to life success? It could be that people higher on PWB behave in specific ways that protect them against illness, such as not smoking, taking exercise, sleeping regularly and complying with instructions when they are given medication. In fact, all these things are associated with PWB but, as Chida and Steptoe showed in their research, the effects of PWB on health remain even when these behavioral differences are fully taken into account. Although the behavior of people with higher levels of PWB does not seem to protect against illness, it certainly does seem that behaviors linked to higher PWB do lead to life success. Lyubomirsky et al. (2005) reviewed a great deal of research and found that higher PWB was associated with a range of behaviors and psychological processes linked to success, including positive self-perceptions, positive judgments of others, performance on complex mental tasks, creativity, flexibility and originality. In addition to the behavioral benefits of PWB the research also suggests biochemical benefits. As the work of Ryff and colleagues, mentioned above, has shown, there are links between certain biochemicals, such as cytokines (e.g. Interleukin 6), which are important for immune system functioning and linked with a range of health outcomes. There are also links with neuroendocrine functions, such as the levels of cortisol (the stress hormone) and PWB (see Box 1.1).

BOX 1.1   **Psychological well-being and the biochemical response**

Many studies have been conducted demonstrating the link between stress and health. However, there is a growing interest in exploring the positive links between PWB and health. A modest pattern of results has been demonstrated to date, specifically in relation to levels of Cortisol and Interleukin 6. Whilst caution should be exercised in placing too much emphasis on the findings due to the relatively small sample sizes (most have also been conducted with older women), it is thought provoking nonetheless.

Cortisol, the "stress hormone", is secreted in high levels in the body's fight or flight response, providing us with a quick burst of energy, heightened memory functions and lower sensitivity to pain among others, preparing the body to respond to perceived stressors. Prolonged levels of Cortisol in the blood, as a result of a failure to relax after a sustained period of high pressure or chronic stress, are associated with negative health outcomes such as impaired cognitive functioning, decreased muscle tissue and increased abdominal fat. Fortunately, there are various techniques that people who find it hard to relax can use to lower the level of Cortisol in their bloodstream (e.g. exercise, listening to music or breathing exercises).

Two recent studies have demonstrated the positive effect of eudaimonic PWB on Cortisol levels. Participants with higher levels of purpose in their life started the day with lower Cortisol levels that stayed lower throughout the day than those with lower levels of well-being (and lower levels of purpose and growth), apparently protecting them from the negative effects of high levels in the bloodstream.

Interleukin 6 (IL-6) is a cytokine, a messenger protein that regulates the body's immune response to disease causing inflammation. Overproduction or inappropriate production of IL-6 is often associated with stress, and in turn high levels of IL-6 are associated with diseases including heart disease, type-II diabetes and some kinds of cancers. This is believed to occur in part because stressed people engage in unhealthy behaviors, e.g. overeating fatty food and smoking which activate the inflammatory response, releasing excess IL-6 into the bloodstream. Studies have also been conducted that demonstrate higher levels of IL-6 in people who have experienced an acute period of psychological stress suggesting it is not just associated with chronic stress.

In relation to the positive impact high levels of well-being might have, there is some early evidence, albeit with a very restricted sample, to suggest that high levels of eudaimonic well-being (purpose in life) are associated with lower levels of the inflammatory response. Quite how this association works is not clear; however, it is an encouraging and developing field of research.

CAUSES OF PWB

Given the likely benefits of higher levels of PWB, it is interesting and rather important to ask – what are the factors that influence levels of PWB? As with most psychological constructs, at the most general level of analysis, there is a simple answer to this question: it is influenced by a mixture of genetics and environment. The genetic influences on PWB seem to operate through personality factors. In other words our genes help to determine our personalities and, in turn, our personalities help to determine PWB. Research has already established that personality factors are heavily influenced by the genes that people inherit from their parents. Psychologists' views of the key factors involved in describing human personality reached agreement about 10 years ago, and nearly all psychologists recognize the so-called Big Five personality factors. These five factors are outlined in Figure 1.3. Each person's standing on these factors becomes fairly clear by about 20 years of age and although there are some changes in later life each person's position on each factor remains fairly stable throughout life. The personality factors are continuous – so everyone lies somewhere between two extremes. For example, on Neuroticism, everyone is somewhere between very emotionally stable and laid back and highly neurotic, tense and anxious.

In fact just under 50 percent of our personality seems to be related to genetic factors. This finding has been established through specific types of research studies – kinship studies. These studies involve people with different degrees of genetic relationship, ranging from twins

---

Big Five

- **Openness**
  intellectually curious, open to new activities, prefer variety and novelty, fantasy and imagination
- **Conscientiousness**
  dependable, prudent, methodical and achievement striving
- **Extraversion**
  gregarious, active, assertive and positive emotions
- **Agreeableness**
  sympathetic to others, cooperative and trusting
- **Neuroticism**
  emotionally unstable, anxious, irritable and depressed

FIGURE 1.3 **The Big Five personality factors**

from a single fertilized egg, who are genetically identical – and usually referred to as identical twins – non-identical twins, born at the same time but two different eggs were fertilized, normal brothers and sisters, through to unrelated people. The studies also take account of whether such people were reared together or separately. The studies then use a combination of data and statistical techniques to estimate how much of a human characteristic is inherited (see Bouchard and Loehlin, 2001; this article provides a fairly non-technical overview of a highly technical area of research). Even though up to 50 percent of personality is inherited that still leaves room for substantial influence from environmental factors: the influence of parenting; life experiences and so on.

Personality is partly inherited, it also influences PWB. Several Big Five personality factors are linked with PWB but the largest effects are that extraversion, emotional stability (low Neuroticism) and agreeableness are all linked to higher PWB. The impact of personality on PWB stretches a long way and even extends to correlations between national personality and levels of PWB. Piers Steel and Deniz Ones (2002) found that personality predicted national levels of PWB even when gross national product was taken into account. In fact, it appears that the influence of our genes on PWB works entirely through our personality factors. Alexander Weiss and colleagues (Weiss et al., 2008) used a sample of 973 pairs of twins and looked at the links between genetic factors and PWB. What Weiss and his colleagues found was that all of the genetically determined variation in PWB was explained by variations in personality factors. So, the only way that our genes affect out PWB is by influencing our personalities. The facts that personality is stable and that it influences our PWB begin to suggest that perhaps PWB is stable as well.

If PWB was entirely determined by personality, then that would be a pretty alarming idea. It would mean that our PWB was not influenced by day-to-day experience or events, that it could not be changed, and that we would be stuck with the fixed level of PWB that we have inherited! Fortunately, personality is only partly determined by our genes, and in turn, PWB is only partly determined by our personality. This means that the net impact of what we inherit on PWB leaves plenty of room for PWB to be influenced by what we do or by the situations we are in.

Of course there are many factors in our situations that might affect PWB but this book is about work and PWB, so let's concentrate on links between work and PWB. The first point to make is that, for most people, work is quite important for PWB. By the time people enter work their personality is more or less set, but, as we know, that does not mean that PWB is also set. In fact, when all other things are equal, people do seem to revert to a "set point" level of PWB that is their normal level of well-being. This set point may be at least partly determined by genetic factors. The role of the set point for PWB is explored more fully in Chapter 4. The critical importance of work for PWB is demonstrated in some research reported by Richard Lucas and colleagues (Lucas et al., 2004). They studied people who became unemployed and then found work again. Unsurprisingly they found that being out of work was linked with lower PWB (there are many other studies to support this result). They also found that when people found work again, their level of PWB moved back toward the set point – but never quite returned to previous levels, suggesting that significant life events can influence our transient and our baseline levels of PWB.

Work is important for PWB and PWB is important for work. As the study mentioned above shows, being forced out of work is distressing and has negative consequences for PWB. Of course, some work is unhealthy and may be damaging to PWB but for the most part, working is good for people. It is worth taking a moment to consider why this is so – what is it that work generally provides that is good for PWB? The obvious answer is money, and of course, that is important.

Earning money enables people to access goods and services that provide both the essentials and the pleasures of life. So, first and foremost, most people's immediate reaction to the question of why do you work would be – for the money (see Box 1.2). But good work provides more than economic reward. A second fairly obvious thing that work provides is a structure and purpose to people's day-to-day lives. As we have seen earlier in this chapter, one of the two key factors in PWB is a sense of purpose and of meaning. For many people work can help to provide this important "eudaimonic" experience. For most people working involves interacting with other people. Sometimes the other people at work may seem less than helpful and a source of reduced well-being, rather than a positive influence. For the most part though, when people respond to surveys about work, their relationships with others feature as one of the positives. A quick look at the factors that make up well-being laid out in Figure 1.1 shows immediately just how many of them could be influenced by what happens in the workplace. For example, it is easy to see how work can provide opportunities for personal growth, purpose in life and positive relationships with others. In turn, as we shall see in the next chapter, people with higher PWB are better workers and deliver important benefits to their organizations.

BOX 1.2 **Well-being and money**

Although many people spend much of their time trying to make more money, having more money doesn't seem to make us that much happier, or provide higher levels of well-being. In fact it is fairly well-reported that the relationship between happiness and money is non-linear. That wealth increases human happiness when it lifts people out of real poverty but that it does little to increase happiness thereafter. Information from global surveys that ask people how content they feel with their lives is one of the best sources of information on this. In a typical survey where people are asked to rank their sense of well-being or happiness on a scale of 1 (not at all) to 7 (completely satisfied) average scores of 5.8 were reported by American Millionaires, Inuits of Northern Greenland and the Masai tribe of Kenya, who I think you'll agree experience differing levels of luxury in their life. Homeless people from Kolkata came in at 2.9 but slum dwellers (one economic rung above the homeless) rate themselves at 4.6, far closer to the American Millionaires.

There are at least two factors that have been identified as playing a part in the above: choice and separating "needs" from "wants". Studies show that choice is important in happiness but again only up to a point, after which it becomes overwhelming and possibly leaves people worrying that they could have chosen something better than they did. Secondly, "wants", things that are nice to be able to afford, have a habit of becoming "needs" (e.g. the Internet) and satisfying needs brings less emotional well-being than satisfying wants. On a positive note, there is evidence to suggest that well-being can be increased by spending money on others, even relatively small amounts.

In terms of salary, one study by Dan Gilbert reported that Americans who earned $50,000 per year were much happier than those who earned $10,000 per year, but Americans who earned $5 million per year were not much happier than those who earned $100,000 per year. Furthermore, life satisfaction appears to be much more strongly related to ranked position of the person's income (compared to people of the same gender, age, level of education or from the same geographical area) than how much money each person earned. More recent findings report that income is more strongly associated with happiness for individuals paid by the hour than by salary due to the impact on feelings of self-worth.

Studies tracking changes in a population's reported level of happiness over time are also an interesting source of information on this subject. Gross domestic product per capita has significantly increased in much of Western Europe, the USA and Japan since World War II, but people's sense of well-being, as measured by surveys has shown only mild improvements. It is believed that some of this is due to technological advances that have a significant lifestyle impact on one generation e.g. the washing machine, that are taken for granted by subsequent generations. This also relates to the idea of the "hedonic treadmill" – see Chapter 4.

CHAPTER 2

FOR ORGANIZATIONS

As Chapter 1 of this book has shown, PWB is important for individual employees in many different ways. Higher PWB is linked to life success, better health, career success, better relationships with others and more. This chapter concentrates on the benefits that high levels of PWB bring to the organization. Let's begin by looking at a few examples in specific sectors.

One of the biggest problems that hospitals in some countries have to face at the moment is the incidence of Methicillin-resistant Staphylococcus Aureus (MRSA). MRSA is a nasty infection that has developed some resistance to antibiotics. For patients with open wounds or with weakened immune systems MRSA is very dangerous and health professionals are interested in finding ways of minimizing its spread. One solution, which has been tried in several countries, including the United States, the Netherlands and Denmark, is to screen patients before admission to hospital. Obviously this can work up to a point, but does not guard against infection acquired while a patient is staying in hospital. Rigorous cleaning of surfaces, gowns and so on and regular handwashing with effective cleansers are essential to minimize the spread of MRSA within a hospital. Anyone about to enter hospital would be interested in the factors that are linked with lower rates of MRSA infection. One link that has been established is between indicators of staff well-being and rates of MRSA infection (Boorman, 2009). The relationship between MRSA infection and staff well-being does not seem to arise because members of staff with lower well-being are likely to be carrying the bacterium (although this is possible and some studies have found quite high levels of staff, more than 10 percent, carrying MRSA). The relationship seems more likely to arise because members of staff with higher levels of PWB behave differently – in ways that are likely to reduce the incidence of MRSA – more about this later.

Manufacturing industry has a very different environment from health care. In this type of work environment there are often quite clear measures of productivity, and competition is such that companies need to do everything that they can to improve the productivity of their employees. One specific factor that has been linked with productivity is whether employees feel that the organization shows concern for their welfare (Patterson et al., 2004). When this is the case the organization can expect to see better productivity levels. Malcolm Patterson and his colleagues looked at results across 42 different manufacturing companies. They found links between various aspects of the psychological climate in the company and productivity measures. Because they had been able to collect data over a period of time, they were able to be fairly confident that the climate factors actually caused changes in productivity. They examined many aspects of company climate and found eight specific factors that predicted productivity – in the year *after* they were measured. Productivity was assessed as the financial value of net sales per employee. As an integral part of the study they also controlled previous productivity, company size and industrial sector. The eight climate factors linked to productivity were: supervisory support, concern for employee welfare, skill development, effort, innovation and flexibility, quality, performance feedback and formalization. Concern for employee welfare (well-being) was the climate factor that showed the strongest relationship with subsequent productivity. So, results from manufacturing industry show that organizations derive benefits from being seen to care about the well-being of their employees.

People who work in service industries are in a sector where the challenges are different again. In any service role that involves dealing with customers it is common for employees to be confronted with customers who are irritated or even very angry. Perhaps they have spent a long time on the telephone helpline holding on, standing in a queue waiting for attention or have arrived late at night at a hotel to find that their booking is not recognized. Employees dealing with these kinds of difficult situations have to think on their feet a great deal. They often need to rely on the support and help of colleagues to solve unexpected problems. To resolve the customers' concerns, the person on the spot and their colleagues often need to "go the extra mile" and do something that is outside the scope of their normal job. Sometimes this type of behavior is referred to by organizational psychologists as good "organizational citizenship" or putting in "discretionary effort".

It may also be referred to as "extra role" behavior – because it often involves members of staff in carrying out tasks that are not strictly part of their normal role. As a customer it can be very frustrating to see simple things that could be done but are neglected because they are not part of someone's defined role. One of the authors well remembers visiting a mainline railway station in the United Kingdom on a regular basis. For several weeks he noticed that in the washroom a hand dryer was not functioning. A simple repair with a piece of tape would have made it serviceable until a proper repair could be carried out. But week after week nobody had taken the initiative to do anything. Probably everyone has many examples of similar things. How angry and frustrated the business' leaders must be to see that their employees are not prepared, or don't feel able, to step outside their specific role and fix a simple problem. But how often do these same business' leaders link the problem to the well-being of their members of staff? Guess what? In service organizations where staff well-being is higher, members of staff are more likely to go the extra mile (Moliner et al., 2008); customer satisfaction and service quality have also been shown to be linked to employee well-being (Leiter et al., 1998; Dorman and Kaiser, 2002).

Given the knowledge that studies have shown links between productivity, customer satisfaction, patient care, service quality and PWB, it is perhaps not surprising that PWB has actually been linked with a very wide range of important outcomes for organizations. First, research has established that PWB is directly correlated with performance. Studies conducted in organizations (Wright and Cropanzano, 2000) have revealed positive relationships between levels of PWB and job performance, demonstrating that people with higher levels of PWB perform better at work than those with lower PWB; indeed, the results show that well-being predicts job performance more effectively than job satisfaction does. Figure 2.1 illustrates the strength of the relationship between PWB and (self-reported) productivity levels. The results in Figure 2.1 come from a sample of 750 employees in the northwest of England – but we have obtained similar results from organizations in many different settings.

As Figure 2.1 also shows, an increase of one point on the PWB scale (which was measured on a scale from 1 to 5) is associated with an increase in productivity of 8.8 percent.

One large piece of research analyzed data from nearly 8000 separate business units in 36 companies (Harter et al., 2003). They found

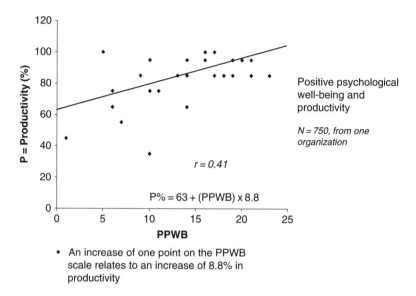

- An increase of one point on the PPWB scale relates to an increase of 8.8% in productivity

FIGURE 2.1 **The relationship between PWB and productivity**

significant relationships between well-being scores on an employee survey and business unit level outcomes, such as customer satisfaction, productivity, profitability, employee turnover and sickness-absence levels. As well as demonstrating links between well-being and important organizational outcomes, their research reports are interesting in another way, as they illustrate the potential relationships between PWB and employee engagement. Although they discuss their work as an illustration of the "well-being" approach in some of their publications, they also refer to the survey that they use as a measure of engagement-satisfaction. The relationships between PWB, employee engagement and job satisfaction are interesting and important and they are explored more fully in the next chapter of this book.

PWB AND "PRESENTEEISM"

Low levels of PWB have obvious consequences for sickness-absence rates in an organization but they also appear to be important when it comes to the interesting phenomenon of presenteeism. Presenteeism is both important and somewhat misunderstood. Let's tackle the misunderstanding aspect first. In practice the term seems to be associated

TABLE 2.1 **Productivity losses due to sickness presenteeism**

Condition	Average productivity loss
Seasonal allergies/Allergic Rhinitis/Hay fever	4.1%
Migraine	4.9%
Depression	7.6%

Source: Hemp, P. Harvard Business Review (2004).

with at least three different meanings. One of these refers to people attending even though they are sick. In practice of course, this is quite common. Many people will still attend work when they have a cold or perhaps an ongoing health condition such as migraine or hay fever. Generally when people are sick they perform less effectively. For example, the results in Table 2.1 show the loss of productivity associated with some of the common forms of illness that do not always prevent people from working.

The second meaning that is sometimes given to presenteeism concerns putting in long hours but not actually working all of the time, or leading people to believe that you are working (e.g. leaving a jacket on the back of a chair) – sometimes referred to as putting in "face time". The third meaning involves working at a reduced level because of other distractions, such as browsing the Internet or playing games online.

As far as research on presenteeism is concerned it is the first type of presenteeism, sickness presenteeism, which has received most attention. Sickness presenteeism due to psychological problems seems to be a particular problem and some reports have estimated that the costs of presenteeism are greater than those due to sickness-absence. The Sainsbury Center for Mental Health (Undated) has estimated that in the United Kingdom in 2006 presenteeism based on psychological health problems accounted for 1.5 times as much working time lost as absenteeism and costs more to employers because it is more common among higher-paid staff. They also estimated that the average cost of psychological health problems per average employee was £1000 pa – with sickness-absence accounting for 32 percent of this and presenteeism 58 percent.

There is little doubt that presenteeism is quite widespread. Table 2.2 shows some prevalence data for presenteeism for a sample of nearly 40,000 employees in the United Kingdom.

TABLE 2.2 **The prevalence of presenteeism**

	Health "Good"	Health "Not good"
No absences	35% (Healthy and present)	28% (Presentees)
Some absences	13% (Healthy but not always present)	24% (Unhealthy and not always present)

As Table 2.2 shows, some 28 percent (about 11,000 people) reported some degree of presenteeism. Levels of presenteeism are associated with a number of other factors and further analysis of the results from the sample reported in Table 2.2 showed that for people who report poorer than average levels of PWB presenteeism is even higher (38 percent).

WORKPLACE FACTORS AND PWB

So, there is a significant amount of research offering support for the idea that organizations in which employee PWB is higher will get better results. Obviously this is important and establishing that higher levels of PWB are linked to important organizational benefits is a key component of the business case for PWB. But once this is established what also becomes important is to understand *how* this relationship works. The research outlined next helps to provide some insights into this.

As well as demonstrating the links between PWB and productivity the researchers who carried out this work also looked at the factors in the workplace that are known to influence employee PWB. Their study (Donald et al., 2005) examined PWB results, across 15 different organizations in the United Kingdom. These organizations were from both the public and the private sector. Two manufacturing plants, a local education authority, a large county council, three police forces, three universities, a prison service and various other service providers were included in the total sample of over 16,000 people. Respondents worked in a range of professional, administrative and manual occupations. The researchers used an earlier version of the well-being survey (ASSET, see Faragher et al., 2004). The survey tool measures a range of factors related to well-being and is explained more fully elsewhere

TABLE 2.3 **Some illustrative factors measured by the ASSET survey tool**

ASSET factor	Explanation
Workplace factor: Control and Autonomy	The items included in ASSET for this factor focus on the extent to which job holders feel that they have control over how they carry out their work – e.g. involvement in decision-making, whether ideas and suggestions are taken into account.
Workplace factor: Work (over)load	The items included in ASSET for this factor focus on the extent to which the workload itself is a source of excessive pressure for an individual – e.g. unrealistic deadlines, unmanageable workload
Organizational outcome: Productivity	This ASSET scale asks people how productive they have felt over the previous 3 months – using a percentage scale – up to 100 percent productive.
Individual outcome: Psychological (ill)health	This scale picks up the extent to which people have experienced common problems – e.g. mood swings, constant tiredness, feeling unable to cope – that are known to be indicators of poor psychological health

in this book (see Chapter 5). For the moment Table 2.3 gives a brief illustration of some of the factors measured by ASSET.

As well as exploring the links between PWB and important organizational outcomes (e.g. this particular study showed that psychological health was linked to individual productivity) research of this kind has looked at the impact that key workplace factors (such as degree of control and autonomy, access to resources and communications) appear to have on psychological health and well-being. The results of this research and other work start to enable us to move beyond a simple statement that higher PWB is linked to better performance, customer satisfaction, organizational citizenship and so on. It enables us to identify the aspects of the workplace that drive levels of PWB. The links between workplace factors and PWB are fully explored in Chapter 7 of this book. The identification of the workplace factors that influence PWB is the first of two very important questions that need to be addressed when considering the role of PWB at work from the perspective of the organization. The second question focuses on how higher levels of PWB lead to the better outcomes for organizations. These two questions are of considerable practical relevance to anyone interested in harnessing the benefits of PWB for an organization. Understanding the workplace factors that influence PWB enables actions to be taken that can improve the PWB of a workforce. Not being clear about the key factors that influence PWB leaves the leadership of an organization in the dark about what to do to improve or maintain the PWB of their employees. Is it best to improve pay, or are supportive work relationships more important? What about freedom and autonomy to do a job in the way an employee thinks is best – is this an important factor in determining PWB?

Researchers have been interested in the workplace factors that influence PWB for decades – and through the research conducted, they have been able to develop a pretty clear idea of the factors that are important. Researchers interested in the impact of workplace factors on PWB initially focused on a few specific factors. These factors make perfect sense from an intuitive perspective. The first factor concerns the demands placed on people at work. When people are confronted with excessive demands, over a long period, PWB is likely to be damaged. This much is fairly obvious but it is really important to recognize that lower demands do not automatically lead to higher levels of PWB. To understand this point, consider how it might feel to go to work and have nothing at all to do – imagine if no one made any demands on you and there was no requirement for you to do anything at all! When asked to consider this scenario most people's initial reaction (especially if they have a busy and demanding job) is to say, "What bliss". When asked to consider how they would feel about this same scenario being repeated day after day the reaction changes – indeed many people say that they would not last long in such a job and would need to move to somewhere where they could feel useful; and, of course, this is the point: it is the demands of work that make us feel worthwhile and useful. Meeting these demands provides satisfaction, especially if they have been challenging. What this means is that the relationship between work demands and PWB is not entirely straightforward. It is certainly not the case that reducing work demands will lead to lower PWB, sometimes the opposite is required and more demanding work will improve people's PWB. This is good news for organizations and it also provides us with another insight into why there is such a good relationship between the PWB of its members of staff and the overall performance of an organization.

Just as it's true that reducing demands does not automatically improve PWB, it is also the case that organizations will not achieve good results by constantly increasing demands on people. The diagram

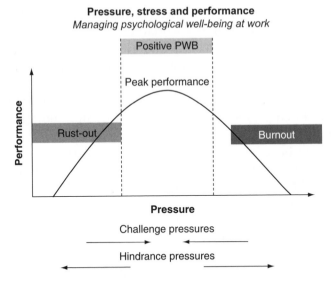

Pressure, stress and performance
Managing psychological well-being at work

FIGURE 2.2 **The pressure performance curve**

in Figure 2.2 illustrates this point. When the pressure (e.g. demands of the job or internal drive to perform) is low, performance will not be at its maximum. As the pressure increases, performance increases but as pressure increases even further it becomes too great – and performance actually begins to suffer. Performance under high pressure may be damaged because the pace of work is too intense, because there are too many things to be done, insufficient resources to do them or a whole range of factors.

Initial research focused on the idea that if people had more control over how they carried out their work, this would enable them to mitigate some of the demands and pressures of the job. For example, high demands and high pressure might be easier to cope with – and even be quite motivating – if you have significant control and discretion over how to do the work. Things like being able to choose times for breaks, working from home/working flexibly, deciding how to go about a piece of work and so on are all part of the general idea of control. The support and resources available to someone have also been proposed as important factors in determining how people respond to work demands. Support from co-workers, support from the boss, resources and equipment and up-to-date information are all examples of workplace factors that have been shown to influence how people respond to work demands. Research to understand how work demands, control, support, resources and other factors all interact to influence PWB is continuing and various theories and ideas are being developed and evaluated. A simple model of the key workplace factors that influence PWB is given in Chapter 7. In particular six core factors are described and related to real jobs and areas of work using examples. The six core factors are: resources and communication; control; work–life balance/workload; job security and change; work relationships; and job conditions. Other important topics covered in Chapter 7 include the impact of management and leadership and the design of jobs and work.

For now, let's return to the primary focus of this chapter – the impact that PWB can have on organizational performance. So far, it should be clear that there are clear links between the PWB of members of a workforce and key organizational outcomes, such as customer satisfaction, patient care, employee turnover and levels of sickness-absence. As we have seen in the previous section of this chapter, specific workplace factors such as control, the availability of resources and work demands are all important in understanding what influences PWB for people at work. Understanding the workplace factors that influence PWB is essential and useful; crucially, it tells an organization that wants to improve the PWB of its workforce which factors are likely to be important. But there is still an important unanswered question about the relationship between PWB and the performance of an organization – why does an organization in which employees have higher levels of PWB perform better? Of course the simple answer to this question is to say that its employees will be more productive, will be sick less often, perform better and relate to customers better. All of that is true but it doesn't really explain what it is that members of staff with higher levels of PWB will do that is different, or why.

It seems likely that the answer to this question lies in the recently developed and rapidly growing field of positive psychology. Historically psychology has been much more interested in negative issues than positive ones. The research literature contains something like 15 times as many articles about negative topics, such as negative emotions (Myers, 2000) compared with positive ones. Negative organizational outcomes have received a similarly disproportionate amount of attention with one of the leading journals in the health psychology field publishing 15 times more articles about negative organizational outcomes, compared with positive ones. The field of positive psychology has been developed partly in response to this overwhelmingly negative mindset. Positive psychology is the study of the conditions and processes that contribute to the flourishing or optimal functioning of people, groups and institutions. It's important to recognize, from the outset, that positive psychology is a serious attempt to develop a scientific and evidence-based approach to this field of study. Positive psychology is most definitely NOT the soft, under-researched, rather unfocused philosophical approach that is associated with being falsely positive, standing in front of a mirror and affirming that you are a wonderful person and so on. The founders of positive psychology are serious scientists who conduct their research with rigour and publish in peer-reviewed journals. Before using the findings from positive psychology to understand how people with higher levels of PWB benefit their organizations, let's get the flavor of this exciting research area by looking at some of the findings that have emerged since its beginnings not much over 10 years ago.

No introduction to positive psychology would be complete without mention of Martin Seligman of the University of Pennsylvania, considered by many to be the founder of the field. Seligman and Csikszentmihalyi (2000) provide a handy summary of some of the interesting findings from positive psychology (see Table 2.4). As they note, many of the findings are not of the "my grandmother already knew it" variety!

There are many links between the research emerging from positive psychology and PWB at work but one of the most important ideas concerns the role that positive emotions and a positive sense of purpose play in building and broadening people's psychological resources. Barbara Fredrickson and her colleagues have carried out

TABLE 2.4 **Some findings from positive psychology**

✓ Women who flashed a Duchenne (genuine) smile in their yearbook photos as freshmen have more marital satisfaction 25 years later
✓ Brief raising of positive mood enhances creative thinking and makes doctors more accurate and faster to come up with the proper liver diagnosis
✓ In business meetings a ratio of greater than 2.9:1 for positive to negative statements predicts economic flourishing
✓ Among 96 men who had had their first heart attack, 15 of the 16 most pessimistic men died of cardiovascular disease over the next decade, while only 5 of the 16 most optimistic died

---

ground breaking research that shows how the experience of positive emotions serves to broaden the scope of people's attention, thought processes and actions. In other words, experiencing positive emotions is not just a fleeting pleasant feeling, the experience actually enhances the way we think and act and improves our psychological capabilities. Next time you have a good laugh remember this, especially if it comes during a difficult meeting or period of work! Further research has also shown that the broadening effect of positive emotions leads to an upward positive spiral (Fredrickson and Joiner, 2002). As Fredrickson and Joiner (2002) put it, "...experiences of positive emotions also increase the odds that people will feel good in the future..."; as predicted by Fredrickson's broaden and build theory, "...this upward spiral is linked to the broadened thinking that accompanies positive emotions" (p. 175). It seems likely that this building of psychological capital may be at the heart of the results that are obtained by organizations that nurture the PWB of their members of staff. People with higher levels of PWB also appear to have better psychological resources – they are more optimistic, more resilient in the face of setbacks and have a stronger belief in their own ability to cope with things (Avey et al., 2010). Some psychologists refer to these qualities, that are associated with higher levels of PWB, as psychological capital – PsyCap for short (see Box 2.1). Although the PsyCap idea has been developed only recently, there has already been research to show that it can be enhanced by the use of web-based training interventions.

BOX 2.1 Psychological capital

High levels of psychological capital (PsyCap) are positively correlated with positive organizational outcomes such as employee satisfaction, performance and effective organizational change as well as lower levels of absenteeism. In line with the "broaden and build" theory, PsyCap also has a self-reinforcing effect on the individual; positive outcomes increase perceived self-efficacy and feelings of hope, and consequently overall PsyCap.

Some of the key factors that have been identified as contributing to overall PsyCap are:

- **Self-efficacy** – having the confidence to take on and put in the necessary effort to succeed at challenging tasks

---

BOX 2.1 **(Continued)**

- **Optimism** – making a positive attribution about succeeding now and in the future (see also Chapter 8)
- **Hope** – persevering toward goals and when necessary redirecting paths to goals in order to succeed
- **Resiliency** – when beset by problems and adversity, sustaining and bouncing back and even beyond to attain success (see also Chapter 8)

It is a useful construct for organizations because PsyCap, measured by the PCQ (PsyCap Questionnaire), can be developed by increasing scores on the four underlying factors.

Simple web-based – microintervention – training programs (typically lasting approximately 2 hours) that aim to develop the four aspects of PsyCap have been demonstrated to do so effectively. At the core of these microinterventions is the philosophy that the training should be highly personalized and interactive.

It seems then that strong underlying psychological resources and good PWB go together. We already know from material covered in Chapter 1 of this book that higher PWB is associated with a range of behaviors and psychological processes linked to success, including positive self-perceptions, positive judgments of others, performance on complex mental tasks, creativity, flexibility and originality. These behaviors and processes are ones that the leadership team of any organization would wish for in their staff. Such behaviors lead more or less directly to some of the positive organizational outcomes that have been shown to be linked to PWB. The picture that emerges then is one where an important network of factors, PsyCap, PWB and positive behaviors and psychological processes are all linked together to provide organizations that nurture the PWB of their members of staff with a range of positive outcomes.

CHAPTER 3

WELL-BEING AND EMPLOYEE ENGAGEMENT

This chapter explains how the important ideas of employee engagement and PWB can be drawn together to provide a powerful combination to benefit employees and organizations alike. Around the world there is currently a great deal of interest in the concepts of employee engagement and employee well-being. The statistics of engagement are interesting and show that improving employee engagement leads to a range of positive outcomes for organizations – they also show that in many organizations the levels of engagement are actually quite low. On a global basis just 21 percent of the employees surveyed around the world are engaged in their work (Towers Perrin, 2007), meaning they're willing to go the extra mile to help their companies succeed, 38 percent are partly or fully disengaged. The relatively low levels of engagement appear to stretch across very different societies and economies. For example, in mainland China, 33 percent of people are reported to be partly or fully disengaged (Towers Perrin, 2007). Engagement levels in the Western economies also appear to be relatively low, with fewer than 20 percent of employees in the United Kingdom reported to be fully engaged and over 40 percent either disengaged or at least "disenchanted" (Towers Perrin, 2007).

Engagement is important because poor levels of engagement translate into poor performance for individual employees and the organization as a whole. There is a large body of evidence showing that when employees are more engaged their organizations do better. One large study showed that business units with employees who score in the top half on engagement are much more successful on a range of indicators than those in the bottom half (Harter et al., 2009). For example, business units with employee engagement scores at the 99th percentile have nearly 5 times the success rate than those at the 1st percentile. The differences between organizations in the top quarter compared with the bottom quarter were: 12 percent in customer ratings, 16 percent in profitability, 18 percent in productivity, 25 percent in turnover (high-turnover organizations), 49 percent in turnover (low-turnover organizations), 49 percent in safety incidents, 27 percent in shrinkage, 37 percent in absenteeism, 41 percent in patient safety incidents and 60 percent in quality (defects).

From the available evidence it seems that organizations with more engaged employees provide a better return for investors, have customers who use their products more, have customers who are more satisfied, lower staff turnover rates, lower absenteeism and perform better financially. Engaged employees are also happier with their organizations and are less likely to want to leave and more likely to tell others positive stories about their organization (an important issue when recruiting future talent). Table 3.1 summarizes some of the relevant evidence (see Attridge, 2009 for more information).

Not surprisingly, given the background research evidence, there is widespread belief amongst HR practitioners that improving and sustaining high levels of employee engagement is good for business. It is interesting that despite this widespread consensus, there is actually very little firm agreement on what exactly is meant by engagement and it is clearly the case that different practitioners make use of a variety of different items and scales to measure what they refer to as engagement. One group of influential researchers defined engagement as, "A positive attitude held by the employee towards the organization and its values. An engaged employee is aware of business context, and works with colleagues to improve performance within the job for the benefit of the organization..." (Robinson et al., 2004, p. ix). With its emphasis on business context, performance and benefits to the organization, this approach suggests a "business outcomes" perspective on engagement, in which employee engagement incorporates – and emphasizes – constructs that are most closely connected with the relevant business outcomes. Robinson et al. (2004) also note that this formulation of engagement contains aspects of two constructs that psychologists have been studying for some time: organizational citizenship and commitment. Organizational citizenship refers to the extent to which employees will behave as "good citizens" inside the organization. Typically this involves doing things like helping out a colleague or trying to solve a problem that is not normally defined as

TABLE 3.1 **Benefits for organizations with engaged employees**

Key benefit to organization	Evidence
Better return for investors	Results from *Fortune* magazine's 100 Best companies to work for showed that these companies returned five times as much to investors as the market in general. (Russell Investment Group, 2007)
Increase in operating income	Companies with high levels of employee engagement had a 19 percent increase in operating income over a three-year period. Those with low levels of employee engagement had declines of 33 percent. (Towers Perrin, 2008)
Lower levels of sickness-absence	Actively disengaged employees miss more than 6 days of work per year. Engaged employees miss fewer than three days on average. (Flade, 2003)
Advocacy of organization as a good place to work	Sixty seven percent of engaged employees actively advocate their organization as a place to work compared with only 19 percent of not-engaged employees. (Flade, 2003)
Customer satisfaction/loyalty	Customer data collected across 24 different studies and 20 different organizations showed positive relationships between employee engagement scores and customer perceptions. (Harter et al., 2002)
Productivity	Engaged employees are more productive (e.g. revenue generated per person). (Harter et al., 2002)
Potential impact on organization's products and services	Eighty-eight percent of fully engaged employees believe they can positively impact the quality of their organization's products and services – only 38 percent of disengaged employees feel the same way. (Towers Perrin, 2007)

part of one's job. Organizational citizenship is also sometimes referred to as "extra role behaviour" – because people go beyond the narrow definition of their role to behave as good citizens. The idea of people "going the extra mile" or giving their "discretionary effort" is often embodied in ideas about engagement and explains why Robinson and colleagues include organizational citizenship in the set of constructs

29

that they see as part of engagement. Commitment to the organization, in terms of working hard, believing in the organization and valuing what it does, is also an established area of study for psychologists. Although Robinson et al. (2004) note that engagement is a broader construct and is not entirely explained by either of these established constructs, there is a popular view of engagement that focuses on "positive" employee behavior and attitudes and appears to relate quite closely to the established psychological concepts of organizational citizenship, commitment and attachment. This "business outcomes" view of engagement has also been described as "Narrow Engagement" (Robertson and Cooper, 2009).

A different view of engagement, taken by some specialists, involves placing more emphasis on how the employee feels when he or she is completely engaged. This kind of approach sees the engaged employee as someone who is immersed in his or her work – sometimes even experiencing a state referred to as "Flow" (Csikszentmihalyi, 1990), a state that involves an intense period of concentration on what one is doing, to the extent that time distorts and seems to pass more quickly and one's awareness of self is minimal or even lost completely. Experiencing flow is an intrinsically rewarding experience. The view of engagement that builds on the idea of flow sees engagement as a pervasive and persistent state, characterized by vigor: (work is experienced as stimulating and energetic and something to which employees really want to devote time and effort); dedication (work is a significant and meaningful pursuit); and absorption (work is engrossing and something on which the worker fully concentrates). This approach sees work engagement as "...a positive, fulfilling, work-related *state of mind* that is characterized by vigor, dedication, and absorption" (our italics, Schaufeli et al., 2002, p. 74). This perspective on work engagement focuses on how employees experience their work and is distinctively different from the business outcomes focus noted earlier. Taking yet another perspective, Macey and Schneider (2008) propose a very broad view of engagement, which sees "engagement" as an overarching umbrella term containing different types of engagement, including trait engagement (i.e. engagement as the expression of an individual's personality traits), work involvement and organizational citizenship. This perspective is much more inclusive and broader than the business outcomes perspective or the view of engagement as a psychological state. Table 3.2 gives examples of different approaches to the concept of engagement.

TABLE 3.2 **Some different approaches to engagement**

Source	Approach
Gallup (Harter et al., 2002)	... the individual's involvement and satisfaction with as well as enthusiasm for work.
Schaufeli et al. (2002)	... a positive, fulfilling, work-related state of mind that is characterized by vigor, dedication and absorption.
Towers Perrin (2003)	... the extent to which employees put discretionary effort into their work, in the form of extra time, brainpower and energy.
Robinson et al. (2004)	... a positive attitude held by the employee toward the organization and its values. An engaged employee is aware of business context, and works with colleagues to improve performance within the job for the benefit of the organization.
Hewitt (2004)	Engaged employees speak positively about the organization (Say); exert extra effort that contributes to business success (Strive); and are attached to the organization and don't want to leave it (Stay)
Stairs et al. (2006)	... the extent to which employees thrive at work, are committed to their employer and are motivated to do their best for the benefit of themselves and the organization.
Macleod and Clarke (2009)	... a workplace approach designed to ensure that employees are committed to their organization's goals and values, motivated to contribute to organizational success and are able at the same time to enhance their own sense of well-being.

By and large the view of engagement that is of most interest to HR practitioners and the leadership of organizations is most closely in line with the definition and approach described by Robinson et al. (2004) and referred to above as "business-focused". As already noted, this approach focuses on employee attachment, commitment and organizational citizenship. These concepts hold interest for employers because they are likely to be most directly involved in driving positive employee behaviors – behaviors that, at face value, show the most obvious links with beneficial outcomes such as more effective performance, greater customer satisfaction and so on.

Typical questions in (narrow) employee engagement surveys are illustrated below:

"The goals of my organization make me feel that my job is important"

"I am committed to this organization"

"My opinions are listened to by my bosses at work"

"I am enthusiastic about the job I do"

"At work, I am prepared to work hard, even when things do not go well"

Adopting this narrow view of engagement is appealing to top leadership teams in organizations and to HR practitioners but there are some serious drawbacks and risks in doing this. Before discussing the drawbacks and risks it will be useful to bring in some more ideas about links between engagement and PWB.

PWB AND ENGAGEMENT

The range of approaches to engagement summarized in Table 3.2 show that engagement is variously seen as something that focuses on whether employees are giving their discretionary effort to the organization, whether they are experiencing positive states while at work, whether they are committed to the organization and so on. Some of the approaches, though by no means all of them, also include reference to aspects that are linked to PWB, such as energy, vigor, enthusiasm and thriving. Even questionnaires that are quite heavily focused on narrow engagement will also sometimes include at least a few items that focus on employee PWB (e.g. "I enjoy my work and I feel happy at work"). Despite the fact that some formulations of engagement do make reference to PWB, it is actually very rare to see any explicit reference to how employee engagement and PWB might be related. Of course, business-focused engagement (strong attachment, commitment and good citizenship) is important for the organization, but in some ways it is less important for employees. There are certainly benefits to employees from being committed to their work and feeling positive about the organization that they work for, but the long-term benefit for employees themselves is more closely linked to their personal PWB than to the overall success of the organization.

32

At its most extreme, the narrow engagement approach risks being seen as something that manipulates employees, solely for the benefit of the organization – to squeeze all possible effort and time out of its workforce. Take another look at some of the approaches to engagement summarized in Table 3.2. Although in practice none of the approaches actually does so, some could easily be seen as encouraging employees to ignore any attempt at work–life balance and (perhaps to the detriment of their health) give everything to the organization. Surely a sustainable approach to engagement must also include specific and substantial recognition of the need to maintain employee well-being. This does not mean an approach that merely tries to avoid stress and the worst negative effects that overworking could bring. Rather, it implies an approach that seeks to take action to support and encourage positive employee well-being. In fact, of course, as Chapter 2 has demonstrated, high levels of PWB amongst a workforce have been shown to be associated with many of the positive benefits, for the organization, that are also linked with high levels of engagement. So, are we saying that employee engagement and PWB mean more or less the same thing? No, definitely not. In fact now is a good time to introduce some clarity about a number of terms that are sometimes used quite casually and are often taken to mean the same thing – when, in fact, it is important to recognize that they are quite different. The primary terms that we want to pin down at this point are engagement and satisfaction.

As we have already seen, "employee engagement" is not really a clear, easily defined concept, with a single agreed definition. Various different formulations of engagement – with quite different meanings – have been discussed above. It should be clear from that discussion that although some of the approaches to employee engagement share common ground with the idea of PWB, none of them has the same meaning as PWB. As we have seen elsewhere in this book, PWB refers to the extent to which people experience positive emotional experiences at work (the hedonic aspect of PWB), within a wider context of positive meaning and purpose (the eudaimonic aspect of PWB); but what about job satisfaction? Is job satisfaction basically the same as some of the meanings of engagement? How closely is it linked to PWB? It is a fairly simple matter to establish that job satisfaction is not really the same construct as employee engagement. The clue is in the name! Job satisfaction is about whether people are satisfied with their jobs or not. This can be applied to satisfaction with the job itself, with co-workers and with management and supervision. It is immediately clear that this is something different from most of the approaches to employee engagement. For example, it is quite possible to imagine someone behaving as a good citizen, being committed to their organization or even dedicated to their work, even though they do not particularly enjoy their job. Obviously, it is more likely that high levels of engagement and high levels of job satisfaction go together – and indeed this is supported by the research which shows that the two factors are correlated – but they are not the same. Job satisfaction has been defined as a "...pleasurable emotional state resulting from the appraisal of one's job experiences" (Locke, 1976). This is not the same as being engaged, although it does share some common ground with the approaches to employee engagement that focus on the emotional state that people experience while working.

The fact that job satisfaction relates to an emotional state also suggests that it shares some common ground with PWB and again this idea is supported by the research evidence which shows that measures of PWB and job satisfaction are correlated. For example, in one study Thomas Wright and Douglas Bonett (2007) measured PWB and job satisfaction for a sample of managers in a large organization on the west coast of the United States. They followed the managers over a two-year period and also collected independent assessments of the managers' work performance from their immediate supervisors. In common with other research, their study showed a reasonably strong correlation (0.37) between PWB and job satisfaction. Of course, this makes sense. The satisfaction, or to use a stronger term "happiness", that people feel with their jobs is part of their overall level of satisfaction with the work place. The positive emotional state that we refer to as PWB is clearly influenced by the emotional reaction that one has to one's job, implying that job satisfaction is an important aspect of overall PWB at work. On the other hand, being satisfied with one's job is only part of the picture. For most people their emotional experience of work is influenced by the job they do but there are other factors of importance too. Some measures of job satisfaction are quite broad and as well as including items about relationships with supervisors and co-workers they also cover general factors such as opportunities for growth and development. Even when such wider factors are included as part of the overall reaction to a job there are yet more things such as corporate social responsibility (what if you knew that your organization was exploiting poor people in other parts of the world), work–life balance, the way that internal communications are handled inside the organization that are clearly not part of the job but still have the potential to influence someone's PWB and so on. So, "job satisfaction" – the emotional response that people have to their job (even when "job" is taken to include quite a wide range of factors) – almost certainly has an important influence on overall PWB but it is a narrower concept.

AN INTEGRATED APPROACH TO EMPLOYEE ENGAGEMENT AND PWB

Improving employee engagement is clearly something that has become a priority for leadership teams and HR staff. It makes sense because, as already noted elsewhere in this chapter, there are plenty of business benefits associated with improved levels of engagement. In the final section of this chapter we aim to show that improving engagement without paying equal, if not more, attention to the well-being of employees is likely to lead to problems. The simplest way to illustrate this point is to consider what might happen in an organization that takes the kind of "business results" view of engagement described earlier. At first sight this way of looking at engagement looks very appealing to top teams in organizations. It gets right to the heart of the issues and concentrates on the aspects of engagement that seem most likely to bring business benefits – things like better organizational citizenship, meaning that employees will be prepared to go the extra mile and give their discretionary effort. This perspective is appealing to the senior management, for obvious reasons, but how appealing might it seem to other members of the workforce? In practice an approach to engagement that takes too narrow a focus on only things that will be of benefit to the organization risks losing the goodwill of members of staff. But actually there are more serious problems than resistance or a negative reaction from staff. The more serious problem is that focusing on engagement and ignoring well-being is not likely to bring about sustainable benefits and may even do damage. The damage could be at many levels. There is the already mentioned problem of a loss of confidence amongst members of staff that the organization has their well-being at heart. This alone can have serious consequences. Even more importantly there are risks that severe problems associated with poor well-being will go undiagnosed and begin to build up and cause problems.

The narrow focus approach to employee engagement runs the risk of ignoring potentially serious problems such as a build up in presenteeism (people turning up for work even though they are unwell, see Chapter 2). This is something that may not cause too many problems in the short-term but as time passes could build up to become a serious issue. The solution to these issues is to incorporate well-being into any work done on staff engagement. Almost all work on engagement in organizations involves using the results of surveys to obtain an indication of engagement levels and how they are distributed across the organization. In general the results of such surveys are benchmarked against a set of normative data that enables an organization to compare its own results with those from other organizations. It makes sense to follow a similar approach to the tracking of well-being – and PWB – in particular. This can be done either by including standardized measures of PWB in the narrower engagement survey or by carrying out a separate survey focused specifically on well-being. Taking an approach that incorporates PWB as well as engagement is likely to pay dividends for everyone involved, employers and their workforces alike. The benefits to individuals of good PWB have been covered in Chapters 1 and 2, so from the point of view of the workforce the gains from improved PWB are transparent. What is not always fully appreciated is that the benefits to the organization of improved engagement are likely to be enhanced if attention is also given to well-being. Some statistical data from over 9000 employees in 12 different UK organizations demonstrate this point. The results are illustrated in Figure 3.1.

Figure 3.1 shows the proportion of productivity that is predicted by a "business benefits" measure of the employees' job and work

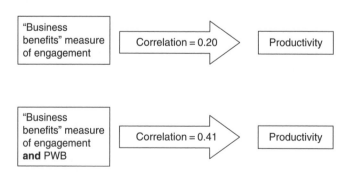

FIGURE 3.1 **The benefits of including PWB as well as engagement**

attitudes (including factors such as organizational citizenship and commitment). The narrow, "business benefits" engagement score does indeed show a good relationship with a measure of productivity; but, importantly, when a measure of PWB is also added the strength of the relationship with the productivity measure increases significantly. What this indicates is that the organization, as well as its workforce, will be likely to get increased benefits by considering PWB alongside engagement.

PART 2

WHAT IS WELL-BEING?

CHAPTER 4

PSYCHOLOGICAL WELL-BEING

PSYCHOLOGICAL WELL-BEING – IS THERE A SET POINT?

How we feel changes over time? Obviously if something bad happens, such as being made redundant or having an accident it will affect how we feel for a while but eventually we will probably recover. Every now and then we seem to "get out of the wrong side of the bed" and start the day in a low and irritable mood for no obvious reason. A disagreement with a colleague or a difficult time with a customer can also affect how we feel.

So far in this book we have been discussing PWB and shown that levels of PWB are related to job performance, physical health, life success, problem-solving and a whole range of factors. Chapter 2 also revealed that the levels of PWB of people in business units is related to the successful performance of those business units, including customers' satisfaction levels and even the share price of the enterprise. These findings seem to suggest that PWB is relatively stable over time – at least stable enough for it to be measured and related to the types of outcomes mentioned above. But that idea seems to be at odds with the fact that we can sometimes feel low one day for no reason at all, or we can have a spat with someone and feel bad for a while afterwards. These thoughts raise the important question of how permanent or temporary PWB is. They also raise the related question of whether everyone has a more or less set level of PWB – and will revert to that level when nothing particularly good or bad is happening to change PWB.

Researchers refer to the idea that we have a fixed level of PWB that we return to as "set point" theory. The idea is based on a similar notion about people's weight – that our weight may fluctuate from time to time due to things like illness, diet or changes of circumstances but in the long run we revert to something close to our set point. Weight is certainly relatively stable over time, although the evidence shows that, for people in general, it varies more as we get older. Weight and PWB are of course very different. For example, although eating more or less will have an impact on our weight, it is certainly not instant – much to the regret of dieters the world over! On the other hand, even during the course of a single day, it's possible to go from feeling really high to really low...and then back again, if the day is turbulent enough! As well as the possibility that PWB may revert to a set point, there is also the idea that when something does change – for better or worse – we become accustomed to the new state of affairs over time and accept things as they are. This idea of the "hedonic treadmill" underpins the notion of a set point by suggesting that the impact of changes in circumstances will not be permanent and we will eventually revert to feeling about the same as we did before the change.

How would you feel if you won the lottery? Common sense (not always a reliable guide of course) tells us that if you had entered the lottery you would be interested in winning – and presumably if you won a jackpot of many millions of pounds that would make you happy. So, at least in the short term you would feel better than before. Anecdotal stories and the occasional feature item in the press provide quite a few stories suggesting that the lot of a lottery winner is not necessarily a happy one and in fact lottery winners sometimes report being even less happy than before. In fact there have been some scientific studies of what actually does happen when people have a stroke of good fortune, such as winning the lottery. In one such study Phillip Brickman et al. (1978) studied people who had won the lottery (in this case the Illinois State Lottery). They also studied a sample of people who had been involved in serious accidents leaving them with paralysis of arms and legs, or from the waist down. They found that although lottery winners did take pleasure from winning the lottery they actually took less pleasure from everyday events and were not significantly happier than a control group who had not won the lottery. These findings were not mirrored by the accident victims though. The accident victims rated themselves as significantly less happy than the controls. Later studies have explored the issues involved more fully and generally such studies do show support for the set point idea and the related concept of the hedonic treadmill – but the findings also suggest that the set point that people have may move somewhat over time. Headey and Wearing (1989) followed a group of Australians over 8 years and like Brickman and his colleagues they found that although people do show a reaction and changes in happiness due to events, they also tended to revert toward their baseline levels. The idea of the hedonic treadmill suggests that permanent changes in our level of happiness are unlikely and that trying to improve our happiness is like running on a treadmill; however hard we run, we only move up for a brief period – and then end up back where we started. For many this would be a rather depressing picture. Presumably it must also mean that our happiness levels are more or less determined by our genetic make-up, with our underlying personality playing a big part in how we feel (Chapter 6 looks at the role of genes and personality in PWB in more detail).

In fact, the true picture seems to be that we do have a set point – but it is not always set in the same place. How happy we feel is, for example, a lot less stable than our height or our weight. Perhaps this is not too surprising but it also seems to be the case that it is less stable than our personality. In fact Frank Fujita and Ed Diener (2005) have shown that it is about as stable as our income and somewhat less stable than blood pressure. Looking at a nationally representative sample from Germany and following them over 17 years, they found that 24 percent of respondents' well-being had changed significantly from the first 5 years to the last 5 years and that stability declined as the period between measurements increased. Almost 9 percent of the sample changed an average of three or more points on a 10-point scale from the first five to the last five years. It seems that there is definitely something in the idea of the hedonic treadmill but it's also true that what happens can also have a lasting effect on how we feel. Many different events can have a lasting impact. Some that have been studied by researchers and shown to have a long-term effect on how we feel include unemployment, marital changes and being involved in a life-changing accident. It also seems likely that different people will be affected in different ways by different events. So perhaps, in life, we are on a hedonic treadmill but if we pedal hard enough or have some outside help it seems that we can move the whole thing up and we are not destined to keep coming back to where we started! (see Box 4.1)

BOX 4.1   **More on set point theory...**

There is a lot of evidence to support set point theory in relation to one measure of well-being (life satisfaction). However, whilst this is true for the majority of people, there does appear to be a group of people to whom it may not apply so rigidly.

One area that we've taken an interest in is research suggesting that personality might play a significant role in whether long-medium term change to reported life satisfaction occurs – specifically the traits "extraversion"(E), "neuroticism"(N) and "openness to experience"(O). The thinking here is that these traits are relatively stable and that the majority of people have mean (average) levels of these three. This manifests itself externally in them continually experiencing life events which are fairly typical or normal for them, and consequently few situations that might be out of the ordinary (either positive or negative). Individuals with high E and O and low N are more likely to encounter an event or chain of events that cause wider fluctuations to reported life satisfaction because of their desire for external and novel experiences. The frequency and intensity of these experiences reinforce each other to raise reported life-satisfaction, which may become permanent.

Research into this is still simple and in its infancy but it's something worth keeping an eye on.

CHANGES IN PWB

Despite the fact that PWB is unlikely to be as slow to change or as stable as our weight, the possibility that it is fairly stable and that there is some pressure to revert to a set point is important. It may have implications for anyone wishing to attempt to improve the PWB of a group of workers for example. The pressure to return to the set point will be working against any attempts to bring about lasting change. At this point it is worth considering what duration of change in how people feel might actually be useful – especially in a work context. To explore the issues involved here it is useful to distinguish between what psychologists refer to as "mood" and "personality" or "disposition". When psychologists refer to "mood" they are referring to how someone feels right now. Mood reflects the ups and downs of our feelings and can change from moment to moment. It certainly may change a few times during any given day, depending on what happens. On the other hand, someone's personality is something that is fairly stable and will not change from day to day. In fact, research in this area has shown that people's personality is fairly fixed once they reach their early 20s. If personality is fixed and stable from someone's early 20s, it is obviously unlikely that work experiences will have much impact on personality. In fact, it is normally the other way round – personality helps to determine people's work experiences. Research has shown that personality is related to the type of jobs that people are best at, the careers that they are likely to choose and also how they behave and feel when they are at work. In terms of how people behave, personality has been shown to predict a range of things including organizational citizenship behavior (see Chapter 3), leadership and overall job performance. Burch and Anderson (2008) provide a review of this research. The links between personality and people's attitudes and feelings are of particular interest in this chapter. The most widely accepted model of human personality is the "Big Five" or Five Factor Model (FFM). Until the FFM was developed personality researchers did not share a clear view of the most important human personality traits. Many different traits were discussed and there were several competing models of personality – none of them accepted by all. The FFM provides the smallest number of broad personality traits that can be used to explain the maximum variation in people's personality. If two traits could be used to explain the variance in personality, psychologists would reduce the FFM to the Two Factor Model (TFM) – but it seems that five factors of personality is the minimum that can be used. A brief description of the five factors (Openness, Conscientiousness, Extraversion, Agreeableness and Neuroticism) – OCEAN) that make up the FFM is given in Figure 1.3 (Chapter 1).

The role of personality in PWB is discussed in more detail in Chapter 6 but for now we need to explore the differences between personality and mood and how these factors relate, in general terms, to PWB. In their work, looking at the stability of well-being over time, Fujita and Diener found that people's satisfaction with their lives as a whole was less stable than their personality characteristics. In effect then we have a continuum of stability that runs from mood at one extreme to stable personality at the other – with PWB somewhere between the two. PWB is a more stable construct than moment to moment mood but it is also more volatile than our underlying personality (see Figure 4.1). To get a useful picture of PWB means focusing more toward the mood end of the continuum, not just how someone is feeling "today". In the next chapter we explain how PWB can be assessed by asking about how people have been feeling over an

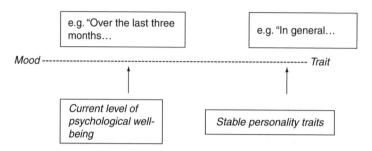

FIGURE 4.1 **Mood, personality and PWB**

extended period of time, such as 3 months. Looking at how people were feeling "right now" would be tapping transient mood to too great an extent. On the other hand, asking people how they feel generally would be going too far toward the personality end of the continuum.

POSITIVE EMOTIONS

As already explained in Chapter 1, PWB has two major components: "Hedonic" well-being, which refers to the subjective feelings of happiness and the less well-known term, "Eudaimonic" well-being, which refers to the purposeful aspects of PWB. Experiencing positive emotions, feeling happy, cheerful, pleased and joyful is a core aspect of hedonic PWB. In fact the experience of positive emotions seems to be an extremely important aspect of our overall well-being and behavior. Of course, it's impossible to go through life on a wave of positive emotions – probably also undesirable as there would be no point of contrast either. We have also seen that the relatively short-term experience of a specific positive emotion is closer to what we refer to as "mood" than PWB. On the other hand, someone who experiences more frequent positive emotions over a period of time is surely experiencing better PWB.

Interestingly positive emotions seem to serve a different function from negative emotions. Barbara Fredrickson explains this by pointing out that negative emotions are triggered by unpleasant, dangerous or even life-threatening situations and they evoke specific, focused reactions to help us to deal with the threat. By contrast, positive emotions are not linked to specific threatening circumstances and they evoke broader, more flexible response tendencies. Fredrickson has developed her ideas about positive emotions into the "Broaden and Build" theory of positive emotions (Fredrickson, 1998). In essence this theory proposes that positive emotions help to *broaden* our range of possible responses and actions – partly because they are not associated with the same threat and urgency to escape them that goes along with negative emotions. According to the broaden and build theory, positive emotions also lead to a building of resources that in turn enables us to cope more effectively over time. There is quite a lot of research to support Fredrickson's theory, suggesting that positive emotions do indeed have the consequences that she proposes. At the most fundamental level there is evidence to show that positive emotions literally broaden people's visual attention. A series of studies has shown that when positive emotions are experienced people's eye movements show broader search patterns with more attention being paid to peripheral stimuli. In fact positive emotions have been linked in experiments to increased receptivity to new information, broader social thinking (people show more imagination and attentiveness in terms of things that they could do for friends) and less racial bias – when positive emotions have been induced white people are more likely to recognize black faces. A few moments' reflection on everyday experiences may help to demonstrate the broadening effect of positive emotions. When things go badly wrong and we get to the edge of panic, what happens? Simple – our attention narrows enormously and we focus more tightly, whether it's on the exit to a burning building or the train that's just about to leave the station. Everyone has had this type of experience and felt the narrowing of attention that goes along with it. How many of us have gone over the same process trying to fix something that doesn't work over and over again, without being able to stand back and get some perspective on the problem? Positive emotions have the opposite effect. Our thinking and hence possible actions become much more expansive and take in a greater range of possibilities. On this basis, the links between positive emotions, PWB and the kind of outcomes reported by Lyubomirsky et al. (2005, see also Chapter 1) such as more effective and innovative problem solving, more positive views of oneself and other people and generally better lives all make sense.

Research on the "Build" aspect of the broaden and build theory is also supportive. For example, in one study participants were trained in a process that helped them to deliberately generate positive emotions. After only a couple of months participants were reporting higher levels of physical wellness and other psychological resources. In more naturally occurring settings positive emotions have also been shown to build resources. After redundancy or bereavement people who experienced more positive emotions (note that they still experienced the normal negative emotions associated with such events) had better well-being a year or so later (for more information, see Cohn and Fredrickson, 2009).

Much of the research on the negative effects of workplace stress supports the idea that prolonged experience of negative emotions depletes psychological resources and makes people more vulnerable to physical and psychological illness, just as the "Whitehall" studies of civil servants in the United Kingdom revealed links between workplace stressors and heart disease (Kuper and Marmot, 2003). Positive emotions appear to have a protective effect by both broadening our range of responses and behaviors and also building our psychological resources, enabling us to cope more effectively. As well as providing a protective effect, positive emotions also help people to bounce back after experiencing adversity (Tugade and Fredrickson, 2004) and they also help to undo the detrimental effects of negative emotions (Fredrickson et al., 2000).

One of the most interesting areas where positive emotions have a beneficial effect is in the promotion of more flexible thinking and creativity. Many laboratory studies have shown how positive emotions can help people to think more broadly and to be more creative in solving problems (for more information, see Isen, 2009). The evidence is not restricted to the laboratory and in one study Teresa Amabile and her colleagues (Amabile et al., 2005) carried out research which looked at diary evidence from over 200 knowledge workers across seven different organizations. On average, they followed people for a period of 19 weeks, collecting data from a daily questionnaire, which included both specific questions repeated each time and free responses from participants. Creativity was measured for each participant by asking peers in the workplace to regularly rate the extent to which the participant had produced novel and useful ideas. They found that people who experienced more positive emotion had better creativity scores.

MEANING AND PURPOSE

As already explained in Chapter 1, PWB actually has two major components. One aspect of PWB (hedonic) is about feeling good and as the discussion above shows feeling good is linked to a range of other positive outcomes and behaviors. The other important aspect of PWB at work (eudaimonic) relates to the meaning and purpose that we associate with our work. Nobody enjoys working at what seem to be pointless tasks day after day. Whatever level of work people do it is important to be able to feel that the work is meaningful and worthwhile. In fact, for people who undertake difficult, dangerous or unpleasant jobs the eudaimonic aspect is particularly important. For a soldier risking his or her life in Afghanistan, feeling that the mission is worthwhile is critically important – the meaning and purpose may be based on supporting colleagues in danger, feeling that helping the Afghan people is worthwhile, believing that the work being done in Afghanistan is keeping the streets of Britain safe or other reasons. Whatever the reasons, without the feeling that it is worthwhile, it is very difficult to sustain high levels of PWB over time. Who is likely to have better PWB – a street cleaner who recognizes the important contribution that the job makes to public health or an office worker in a clean and warm office whose main job involves keeping detailed records that he or she believes no one will ever look at?

Hedonic well-being is about experiences of satisfaction and happiness and – as we have seen in various other parts of this book – such experiences are very important. The eudaimonic dimension of well-being is about mastery of the environment, autonomy and other factors that enable us to feel that what we are doing has meaning and purpose. Just like hedonic well-being, eudaimonic well-being is also associated with important behaviors and outcomes. Indeed, some studies have shown that euadaimonic well-being can have even more significant consequences for health than the positive emotions associated with hedonic well-being, as the study by Carol Ryff and colleagues (described in Chapter 1 of this book) shows.

To return to the question posed at the beginning of this chapter (does PWB have a set point?), it may be that eudaimonic factors are particularly important in pushing people back toward a set point. The feeling of satisfaction that comes with achieving a goal, or the feelings of "flow" associated with being completely engaged in an enjoyable and rewarding activity are part of eudaimonic well-being. In most cases the positive feelings associated with reaching a goal are likely to dissipate over time, and we need to set, and achieve, a new goal to repeat the positive experience. If this doesn't happen we are likely to slip back toward the previous level of PWB. Roy Keane, the Manchester United footballer, made news when he said that the good feelings from winning the championship lasted for a very short time – and then he was focused on the next season and winning it all over again! Everyone has similar experiences, the new job that seemed like a career goal becomes only the next step on the career ladder, the new car, qualification, house and so on. Even "flow" experiences are likely to become less satisfying as we become more familiar with the activity or develop a level of skill that begins to make it less challenging – and we may slip back toward the previous level of PWB. The solution, of course, is Roy Keane's route: set a new and challenging goal. In this way we may be able to avoid the constant return to the set point of the hedonic treadmill and, as Alan Waterman (2007, p. 612) has put it, "...climb the eudaimonic staircase". As we shall see in later chapters the idea of challenging work and the benefits of positive pressure is very important in creating work and a working environment that are conducive to positive PWB.

CHAPTER 5

MEASURING WELL-BEING AND WORKPLACE FACTORS

It's clear from elsewhere in this book that improving the PWB of people at work brings a wide range of benefits, to them as individuals, to their organizations – and of course to wider society. Later chapters look at how the PWB of a workforce can be influenced and enhanced. A prerequisite for changing anything, in a systematic way, is being able to measure it. If you can't measure, it's impossible to know whether things have changed or not. In fact, being able to measure is important, not just for understanding what might change after an intervention but, in the case of PWB, accurate measurement is even more important in deciding what needs to happen to improve things. As well as measuring current levels of PWB, an assessment of the factors that are influencing PWB, the "drivers" of well-being, is an essential measurement prerequisite. A full explanation of the drivers of well-being is covered in a later chapter (Chapter 7) but in this chapter, as well as discussing the measurement of PWB itself, we also discuss some of the core workplace drivers of PWB and how they too can be measured.

Some techniques that do not involve self-report questionnaires have been developed to assess well-being but these methods are not well-established and there is little good quality research to underpin them. By far the most widely used and successful method for measuring PWB is to use self-report questionnaires. In general, the available questionnaire measures of PWB are quite varied and are often based on different underlying assumptions and theories. The distinction between hedonic and eudaimonic approaches to PWB, described earlier in this book (see Chapter 1), is a good starting point for thinking about measures of PWB. As already explained in Chapter 1, PWB has two major components: "Hedonic" well-being, which refers to the subjective

51

feelings of happiness and the less well-known term, "Eudaimonic" well-being, which refers to the purposeful aspects of PWB.

ASSESSING PWB

Let's begin by looking at approaches to the measurement of PWB that take a predominantly hedonic perspective. One approach to measuring hedonic well-being concentrates on what people *think* about specific factors, such as "life" or "work". Measures of job satisfaction or life satisfaction are a good illustration of this. In this approach people are asked to consider (think about) something in particular, such as their work or their life in general and make a considered appraisal of it. Another approach focuses much more on how people *feel* and involves trying to get closer to their emotional (affective) reactions, rather than seeking a more thinking-based (cognitive) evaluation. Although the two approaches are rather different and most investigators tend to use one or the other, there are some questionnaires that use both.

By and large the assessment of hedonic PWB is pretty close to the general assessment of "happiness". Probably the most widely used scale that takes a thinking-based approach is The Life Satisfaction Scale (Diener et al., 1985). This scale contains five items asking about people's level of life satisfaction, for example, "the conditions of my life are excellent", and has been used and validated in many countries. The Oxford Happiness Inventory (OHI) and the related Oxford Happiness Questionnaire (OHQ) (Hills and Argyle, 2002) are more extensive scales developed in the United Kingdom. The OHI is based on the design and format of the Beck Depression inventory (Beck et al., 1961). Each item is presented in four incremental levels, for example, "I am not particularly optimistic about the future, I feel optimistic about the future, I feel I have so much to look forward to, I feel that the future is overflowing with hope and promise." The OHQ includes similar items to those of the OHI (e.g. "I feel that life is very rewarding"), each presented as a single statement which can be endorsed on a uniform six-point scale – Strongly Agree...Strongly Disagree.

As far as affective (feeling-based) assessments of well-being are concerned, the Positive and Negative Affect Scale (PANAS, Watson et al., 1988) is widely used. This assessment contains two self-report scales consisting of ten words describing positive and negative emotions (e.g. upset, enthusiastic, nervous). Participants are then typically asked to provide a rating on the extent to which they generally felt each emotion on a five-point scale ranging from "very slightly" (= 1) to "extremely" (= 5). The validity evidence on this measure is quite good (see Wright and Bonnet, 1992; Wright and Cropanzano, 1997).

ASSESSING EUDAIMONIC PWB

Carol Ryff and her colleagues (e.g. Ryff and Keyes, 1995) take a more eudaimonically orientated approach to PWB, with a model that encompasses six distinct dimensions:

- **Self-acceptance** – a positive view of oneself and one's current and past life
- **Positive relations with others** – warm, affectionate relationships with others
- **Autonomy** – self-determination and freedom, able to resist the influence of social norms
- **Environmental mastery** – a sense of mastery over the environment and everyday affairs
- **Purpose in life** – goals, meaningfulness and a sense of direction, in life
- **Personal Growth** – continuing change, development and psychological growth.

Ryff and Keyes (1995) developed a scale to measure all six of the factors, although subsequent research has suggested that not all of the factors are necessary and eudaimonic well-being may perhaps be explained with a smaller number of factors (Springer et al., 2006).

MEASURING WORKPLACE PSYCHOLOGICAL WELL-BEING

It is clear that any comprehensive assessment of workplace well-being would need to cover both affective and cognitive appraisals of hedonic well-being *and* an indication of the extent to which people experience a positive sense of purpose at work (eudaimonic PWB). This implies that an effective measure of PWB at work should therefore tap: (i) the affective state that people experience at work (related to, but broader than satisfaction with the job itself) and (ii) the extent to which they experience the kinds of eudaimonic factors embodied in Ryff's six dimensions of eudaimonic well-being in their work. This leads to the rather technical definition that we use for PWB as the *affective and purposive psychological state that people experience while they are at work*. In practice what this means is that PWB refers to whether people feel good or not at work (the affective psychological state) and whether they feel that their work is meaningful and has a purpose (the purposive psychological state). From a measurement perspective one final factor needs to be considered – that of the time horizon. The time horizon is important because the stability of the feelings that people experience is important in distinguishing between different types of psychological constructs such as moods and personality traits. As explained in Chapter 4, a good measure of PWB at work needs to strike a middle ground between personality and mood. Asking questions that pick up how people normally feel most of the time would be more of a "personality" measure than a measure of PWB. It would be heavily influenced by people's underlying personality characteristics, rather than their work experiences. On the other hand, asking about how people feel right now would merely tap their current mood, which could change several times, even within the same day!

Although there is a strong literature on the assessment of PWB, relatively little of this focuses on PWB at work. From time to time researchers have used specific sets of questions to measure the PWB of people at work. Cropanzano and Wright (1999), for example, used an index originally reported by Berkman (1971). This asked "how often" respondents experienced specific feelings, ranging from negative feelings, for example, "depressed or very unhappy", through to positive feelings, "on top of the world". This approach clearly takes a hedonic approach to PWB by focusing on affective states. As we have already noted, a comprehensive assessment of PWB at work would need to focus on both hedonic and eudaimonic aspects of PWB.

In this book we focus on the ASSET model for measuring and understanding the role of PWB in the workplace. At the time of writing, we are not aware of any other models for the measurement of PWB at work that are as well-developed as ASSET. The original ASSET questionnaire was derived as a stress audit and focused heavily on psychological ill-health, rather than PWB. Researchers have provided good evidence concerning the psychometric properties of the original ASSET questionnaire (see Johnson and Cooper, 2003; Faragher et al., 2004). In our more recent work on PWB we have enhanced the original ASSET

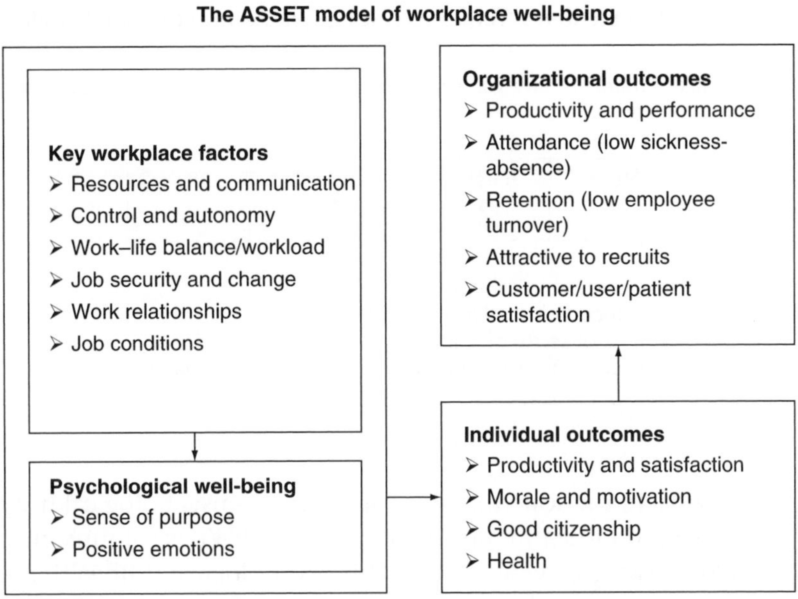

The ASSET model of workplace well-being

Key workplace factors
➢ Resources and communication
➢ Control and autonomy
➢ Work–life balance/workload
➢ Job security and change
➢ Work relationships
➢ Job conditions

Organizational outcomes
➢ Productivity and performance
➢ Attendance (low sickness-absence)
➢ Retention (low employee turnover)
➢ Attractive to recruits
➢ Customer/user/patient satisfaction

Psychological well-being
➢ Sense of purpose
➢ Positive emotions

Individual outcomes
➢ Productivity and satisfaction
➢ Morale and motivation
➢ Good citizenship
➢ Health

FIGURE 5.1 **The ASSET (2010) model**

organizational audit questionnaire to measure positive PWB at work, by developing a set of items to tap both positive emotional experience (i.e. the hedonic perspective) and sense of purpose (i.e. the eudaimonic perspective).

The ASSET model and the key constructs measured are shown in Figure 5.1.

THE ASSET MODEL

The ASSET model shows how a set of specific workplace factors (e.g. resources and communications, control and work relationships) play a key role in determining employees' levels of PWB. The model also shows how, in turn, levels of PWB influence outcomes – both individual and organizational. In Chapter 7 of this book the workplace factors that impact on PWB are fully explained.

As far as the measurement of PWB at work is concerned, the ASSET model incorporates a variety of approaches. The original versions of ASSET took a stress perspective and hence focused on the risks to psychological health from psychologically unhealthy workplaces. Because

TABLE 5.1   **Sample items from the ASSET psychological (ill)health scale**

Over the last 3 months, have you experienced any of the following symptoms or changes in behaviour?			
Never	Rarely	Sometimes	Often
1	2	3	4

- Constant irritability
- Difficulty in making decisions
- Loss of sense of humor
- Feeling or becoming angry with others too easily

of this approach, the scale that was used to assess psychological health actually assessed ill-health, rather than positive PWB (see Johnson and Cooper,2003; Faragher et al., 2004). This psychological (ill)health scale was designed along the lines of other similar scales that were in use at the time (e.g. the General Health Questionnaire) and included items that tapped minor psychological health problems – an accumulation of poor scores on such items would indicate poor overall psychological health, with a possibility of more serious psychological health problems developing over time. An illustration of the items used in this scale is given in Table 5.1.

Scales such as this are useful and can play a key role in measuring risks to PWB and provide a good indication of potential problems, especially when, for example, specific units or sections within a larger workforce show poor scores. In the United Kingdom the Health and Safety Executive (HSE) has developed an approach to the assessment of psycho-social risk in organizations. Again, starting from a stress perspective and seeking to minimize risks, the HSE has developed a measurement questionnaire for use by organizations. Their approach does not provide a direct measure of PWB or psychological health but focuses on the workplace risk factors that can cause psycho-social problems at work. Because of this focus on the workplace drivers of well-being the HSE approach is discussed in Chapter 7, when the key workplace factors that influence PWB are considered.

Avoiding psychological health problems is obviously important for any organization but increasingly the progressive organizations have the additional goal of enhancing the positive well-being of their

TABLE 5.2 **Sample items from the ASSET positive PWB scale**

*For the terms below, indicate the extent to which you have felt like this **during the last three months – at work***

Very slightly	A little	Moderately	Quite a bit	Very much
1	2	3	4	5

- Inspired
- Alert
- Excited

employees. As shown elsewhere in this book there are significant benefits for both employers and employees in building positive PWB, rather than merely avoiding risks. The more recent versions of ASSET therefore also incorporate some items that focus on positive PWB, from both a hedonic and eudaimonic perspective. For example, one set of items, illustrated in Table 5.2 covers the hedonic aspects of positive PWB.

For these items the employee is invited to focus on how they have felt over the last three months at work. This wording is extremely important. To ensure that the response is not merely a reflection of how the person is feeling at that moment a timeframe of the last three months is selected. This also guards against the reply being influenced too heavily by underlying, stable personality factors – which would be more likely if the question focused on how someone feels in general – rather than for a more specific period of time. The use of the term "at work" is also of obvious relevance and focuses the item on how people feel at work, rather than other aspects of their lives.

Assessing the full range of eudaimonic PWB in a work context would require a substantial set of items focused on several of the factors identified by Carol Ryff (see above). This would imply a questionnaire with quite a large number of items. Bearing in mind the importance of also obtaining a measure of the key drivers of PWB, as well as PWB itself, the ASSET approach to the eudaimonic aspect of PWB takes a very focused approach. The items included in ASSET to assess the eudaimonic aspect of PWB at work revolve around the goals of people's jobs and the extent to which their goals are clear, challenging and motivating. As well as drawing on research and theory concerning PWB the items used in this section of ASSET also draw heavily on Goal-setting theory (see Box 5.1) (see Locke and Latham, 2002, for a summary of the relevant research findings and practical applications).

BOX 5.1 **Goal-setting theory**

Many people reading this book will be familiar with Goal-setting theory. It's certainly not new but it is one of the most enduring and practical theories of motivation that psychologists have developed.

The five principles of goal-setting (and some top tips to get started) are:

1. Clarity. When goals are clear and specific, with a definite time set for completion, they are more effective in stimulating performance.
2. Challenge. People are often motivated by achievement. If a goal is easy and not viewed as very important, then it is unlikely to elicit a lot of effort. When you know that what you do will be well-received, there's a natural motivation to do a good job. Rewards commensurate with the level of achievement can boost enthusiasm further.
3. Commitment. Goals must be understood and seem worthwhile if they are to be effective – the harder the goal, the more commitment is required.
4. Feedback. Feedback provides opportunities to clarify expectations, adjust goal difficulty and gain recognition. It's important to provide benchmark opportunities or targets, so individuals can determine for themselves how they're doing. This is particularly important for maintaining motivation for long-term goals.
5. Task complexity. Make sure that the conditions surrounding the goals don't frustrate or inhibit people from accomplishing their objectives – after all they aren't going to be motivating if they do!

You'll see that goal setting is much more than simply saying you want something to happen. Unless you clearly define exactly what you want and understand why you want it in the first place, your odds of success are considerably reduced. Our five top tips are:

1. Set goals that motivate you
2. Set SMART goals (specific, measureable, attainable, realistic and time-bound)
3. Write them down
4. Make an action plan
5. Persevere

TABLE 5.3 **Sample eudaimonic items from ASSET**

Strongly disagree	Disagree	Slightly disagree	Slightly agree	Agree	Strongly Agree
1	2	3	4	5	6

- My job goals and objectives are clear
- I am committed to achieving the goals of my job

Although not without its critics (see Ordonez et al., 2009), the research based on goal-setting as a motivational tool in organizations is extensive and does provide strong evidence that setting clear, specific goals to which people feel committed is one of the surest ways of improving performance and achieving work-related goals. Some sample items used in this section of ASSET are given in Table 5.3.

MEASUREMENT BENCHMARKS AND NORMS

If an HR director was given scores for his or her organization on the type of items in Table 5.2, how would he or she interpret them? Let's say that when asked to rate six positive adjectives like those given in Table 5.2, the average score for a group of employees came out at three. Should the HR director be pleased or disappointed with that score? One way of looking at the scores would be to concentrate on the actual (raw) score. A score of three would indicate that, on average, over the last three months at work, the group of employees involved felt inspired/alert/excited and so on more than "a little" of the time, but they didn't feel like this "quite a bit of the time". Obviously it is possible to assign some meaning to results like that. For example, you could feel quite disappointed that people did not experience the positive emotions described by the adjectives "very much" of the time and that you would have liked to see better scores. If, however, you were told that the average score for tens of thousands of working people in the general working population was fewer than 2, this would probably make you re-evaluate the significance of a score of 3 and feel better about it. So, when looking at scores for indicators of PWB (and many other psychological assessments in fact), as well as knowing the actual score, it is also useful to know how this compares with the scores of

59

similar groups of people elsewhere. The use of "norms", or "norma-tive" comparison groups, provides a simple way of benchmarking any set of scores so that they can be interpreted more clearly.

A simple way of doing this would be to do exactly what was done in the example above: provide a raw score and then give the mean score for the norm group. In practice, this gives some information but not enough. It enables you to see if the raw score is above or below average for the norm group but of course it would be even more useful to know how much better or worse than the norm group the raw score is. A very effective and widely used way of enabling comparisons with norm groups involves converting the raw score to a standardized score that provides a direct comparison with the norm. As long as there is a size-able normative comparison group available to provide the benchmark, such conversions are easily done. In essence that involves making cal-culations to see just how far above or below the norm group mean any specific raw score falls – and then using some form of standard scoring system to indicate this. For example, Standard Ten (Sten) scores show where the actual score is located, in comparison with the norm group, on a ten-point scale. A Sten score of 5.5 means that the actual score is exactly on the mid-point for the norm group. Figure 5.2 shows a selection of normative scoring systems that can be used to provide an

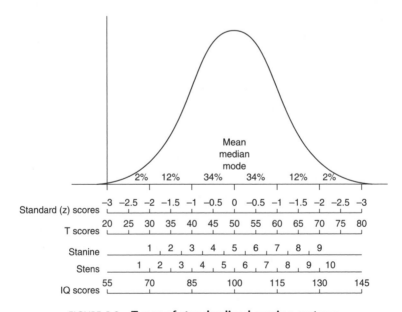

FIGURE 5.2 **Types of standardized scoring systems**

accurate picture of where a score falls in comparison with a normative group.

As well as enabling you to see if any particular raw score is near the mean, above or below the mean for the norm group, converting raw scores to standard scores also provides an accurate view of how far above or below the mean a score lies. This is done by indicating what proportion of the norm group would fall above or below the observed score. For example, a "T" score of 50 is exactly on the mean for the norm group. A "T" score of 60 is greater than 82 percent (2+12+34+34) of the norm group. Similarly a Sten score of 3.5 is lower than 82 percent of the norm group. One key point to notice about all of these normative scoring systems is that as scores move up (or down) the scale, the differences in the number of people falling into the relevant band are not even. For example, Sten scores between 5.5 and 7.5 (a Sten score difference of two points) include 34 percent of the normative group, whereas scores between 7.5 and 9.5 (also a Sten score difference of two points) only include 12 percent of the norm group. What this means is that the higher or lower the scores go on a standard scale, the more unusual the scores become.

Figure 5.3 shows a set of Sten scores for the results of an ASSET survey. It is easy to see from these scores even in black and white (actual scores would be in color) which ones are similar to the norm, which

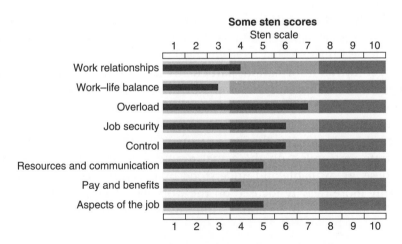

FIGURE 5.3 **Scores from a well-being survey using Stens**

Note: The higher the score, the greater the extent to which the area is troubling people – compared to general working population

scores are different from the norm – and whether they are better or worse than the norm.

OTHER APPROACHES

The self-report questionnaire approach is the only realistic method for collecting reliable information about levels of PWB within an organization. This is particularly the case for larger organizations of a few thousand people and more. The results from the questionnaire can be viewed for the whole organization and also for sub-units, departments, divisions and so on. Questionnaire results can provide a very clear picture of both well-being levels and the drivers of well-being in an organization, especially when the results can be compared with a relevant norm group. In many cases it may be helpful to supplement the questionnaire results with information obtained from talking to members of staff in the organization. One approach to collecting additional information could be to use the telephone. In practice there seem to be good reasons for using this approach only when other options are not available – for example, when staff in an organizations are widely distributed geographically. The research certainly suggests that PWB is better measured using self-report questionnaires distributed by mail or online, rather than by the use of telephone (Springer et al., 2006).

Usually additional information is best gathered after the questionnaire results are available and have been analyzed. The discussions can then focus on issues that have emerged from the questionnaire results and get further information, particularly about follow-up actions that might be desirable. Because of the often sensitive nature of the questions that need to be discussed, it is often a good idea to organize groups of people (focus groups) from across the organization for these discussions. In practice the focus group discussions do not usually concentrate very much on the actual results from the survey – as long as these are available and understood by everyone. The discussion is usually more heavily focused on the workplace factors that influence PWB – and what can be done to improve/sustain things.

PART 3

WHAT INFLUENCES
WELL-BEING?

CHAPTER 6

THE WHOLE PERSON AND PSYCHOLOGICAL WELL-BEING

In a remarkable article, published in 1989 (see Arvey et al., 1991), Richard Arvey and his colleagues produced results that appeared to show that job satisfaction is inherited! At face value this is a very peculiar result indeed because, as we saw in Chapter 3, job satisfaction is supposed to be an appraisal of how we feel about our job. How can this be inherited? Arvey and his colleagues carried out a classic type of study that is used by researchers who are interested in inherited characteristics – a kinship study (see also Chapter 2 of this book). In these studies researchers focus on naturally occurring examples of people who vary from being very closely related, such as identical (monozygotic) twins who are from the same fertilized egg and hence genetically identical, through to unrelated pairs of people. They also take into account whether the people shared a common environment or were brought up apart – as in the case of twins separated from each other at birth and raised separately. This provides an array of people who have varying degrees of genetic and environmental similarity. At one extreme there are identical twins reared together who have common genes and environment. At the other extreme there are unrelated people reared apart who do not share a common environment or genetic background. Careful statistical analysis, taking account of the genetic and environmental similarity, can then reveal the extent to which various characteristics appear to be inherited or environmentally determined. Clearly, the expectation for job satisfaction would be that the environment (i.e. the job that people work in) would determine job satisfaction – but that was not what Arvey and his colleagues discovered. They found that people's genetic background explained a reasonable amount of the variance in their levels of job satisfaction. Their results have subsequently been replicated by other researchers, so we know that it is a stable finding and not a freak result.

It seems almost incredible that people could inherit genes that determine job satisfaction – that would be a very specialized set of genes indeed! In fact, what seems to be happening is that people's genes have some impact on their underlying personality and, in turn, personality has an impact on the levels of satisfaction that people report. Think about the people that you know reasonably well and consider how they react to different experiences. It's likely that you will feel that some people are generally more inclined to be positive about an experience, regardless of what it actually is – and some people might be more inclined to find fault. For example, imagine if several of your friends went on the same holiday. Would it be likely that if they were asked to complete a questionnaire about the holiday, some would almost certainly give more positive scores than others – even though they've had more or less the same experiences? This is exactly what the results from research also reveal, and it is the key to understanding the results of Richard Arvey's research.

The underlying personality that people have helps to determine their reactions to events and experiences. A moment's thought will demonstrate the truth of this point. For example, when something new comes up, some people are likely to react with apprehension and worry, while others are excited and enjoy the variety. In the case of the genetic link with job satisfaction it seems that underlying personality is partly determined by genetic factors, and in turn underlying personality has an influence on how positive people feel about their job – regardless of the job itself. One of the personality characteristics known to have a reasonably strong genetic component is a person's tendency to experience positive emotions. Being more likely to experience positive emotions would obviously make it more likely that someone would feel better about their job, compared with someone less likely to experience positive emotions – even when both work in the same role. So, in other words, people don't inherit genes that determine job satisfaction but they do inherit genes that determine their tendency to experience positive emotions. This finding also raises some very important points about PWB in the workplace. As earlier chapters in this book have demonstrated, PWB is closely related to job satisfaction. Is it likely then that personality rather than workplace factors determines people's levels of PWB at work? Obviously this is an extremely important question because if personality is the main influence on PWB, improving the workplace will be of only limited effectiveness in enhancing PWB. We will return to this point later in the chapter.

PERSONALITY AND PWB

Understanding the relationships between personality and PWB requires a grasp of personality psychology and of the research that links personality with PWB. The psychology of personality is basically an attempt to understand what makes one person different from another. Personality traits are seen as stable predispositions to behave that help to distinguish one person from another. So, someone with an extraverted personality trait has a predisposition to behave in an outgoing way. Figure 6.1 shows how underlying personality translates into specific behavior.

The diagram in Figure 6.1 does not mean that my extraverted acquaintance will definitely come to my party, merely that, in general, all other things being equal, he or she is more likely to do so than someone who is less extraverted. One of the important questions for which psychologists have been able to come up with a reasonably good answer is, "How many underlying personality traits are there – and what are they?" As already explained in Chapter 4, until the FFM of personality was developed personality researchers did not share a clear view of the most important human personality traits,

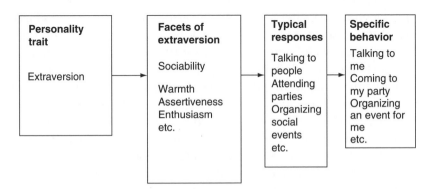

FIGURE 6.1   **The impact of underlying personality on behavior**

or how many there were. Many different traits were discussed and there were several competing models of personality – none of them accepted by all. The FFM provides the smallest number of broad personality traits that can be used to explain the maximum variation in people's personality. If two traits could be used to explain the variance in personality, psychologists would reduce the FFM to the TFM – but it seems that five factors of personality is the minimum that can be used. The five factors (Openness, Conscientiousness, Extraversion, Agreeableness and Neuroticism – OCEAN) that make up the FFM are described briefly in Chapter 1 (see Figure 1.3) and discussed again in Chapter 4.

Research has revealed that there are quite strong relationships between personality factors and PWB (DeNeve and Cooper, 1998), the most prominent relationships being between Neuroticism (negatively related to PWB), Extraversion and Agreeableness (both positively related). The links between personality and well-being are strongest when the hedonic (see Chapter 4) aspects of well-being are considered. This is easy to understand since measures of hedonic well-being, such as Diener's Satisfaction with Life Scale (Diener et al., 1985), are also orientated to people's emotional reactions and evaluations. To get a better understanding of how measures of personality relate to measures of PWB it helps to look closely at the items that are used to measure both types of construct. Table 6.1 shows some of the typical items used to assess both PWB and personality traits of neuroticism and extraversion.

It's interesting to compare the items in Table 6.1. One thing that's noticeable is that some of them seem to be rather similar and could go into either a scale to assess personality or a scale to assess well-being. Obviously the items from some personality scales, such as facets measuring conscientiousness, do not look particularly like the types of items used in well-being scales. But for the personality traits that we know are related to well-being (e.g. extraversion and neuroticism) there are many items that seem quite similar. Perhaps it's not surprising then that there seem to be quite strong relationships between some personality scales and some measures of well-being when the items used to measure both constructs are so similar! In many ways the differences between some personality scales and scales to assess well-being are only a matter of how the items are phrased.

The research evidence points quite firmly to both extraversion and neuroticism as the key personality factors that are involved in

TABLE 6.1   **Items from personality and well-being scales**

Personality Trait – typical types of item	Well-being – typical types of item
Extraversion ■ I am a cheerful person ■ It doesn't take much to make me laugh out loud ■ I enjoy parties with crowds of people	■ I am happy with my life ■ I generally have a good time when I'm with other people ■ I don't have much to look forward to in life ■ My life is not really how I'd like it to be
Neuroticism ■ I get discouraged when things go wrong ■ I often feel cross with other people ■ I am a worrier	
Conscientiousness ■ It's important to me that things are kept tidy ■ I do my best to be dependable ■ I prefer to think things over before acting	

determining levels of PWB. It is interesting to examine this finding and explore more closely why it is these two factors in particular that are most strongly related to PWB. First let's look at extraversion. Most people's idea of the extraverted person focuses on the social aspects of extraversion – in other words the extravert is generally seen as someone who is friendly, outgoing and gregarious. Social extraversion is certainly part of the overall construct of extraversion but extraverts tend to have other characteristics as well. There are many people in public life, such as politicians, who manifest most of the aspects of extraversion. When people meet leading politicians like Bill Clinton or Tony Blair they often talk about how warm and positive they were – as well as seeming to be gregarious and friendly, with a strong "presence". All of these characteristics illustrate the broad concept of extraversion – as well as being friendly the classic extravert is also likely to be enthusiastic, warm and positive. It's fairly easy to see how these underlying personal characteristics translate into an overall enhanced level of positive PWB. That's not to say that extraverts never feel low or even experience periods of depression – if the situation is negative and severe enough anyone will be affected. But, in general, the positive emotionality linked with extraversion (rather than the facets related to social extraversion) are likely to support generally higher levels of positive PWB.

Neuroticism is sometimes seen as being more or less the same as being anxious – and is associated with being "nervous". As with extraversion, this view of neuroticism is true but only part of the picture. Neuroticism is related to emotional instability and as well as being prone to anxiety people who are high on neuroticism also tend to experience negative emotions more easily and to feel low more easily. In general, they also find it more difficult to regain a positive outlook after negative experiences. Again once these facets of neuroticism are understood it is reasonably easy to see how the trait may be linked to lower levels of PWB.

PERSONALITY AND THE SET POINT FOR PWB

In Chapter 4, the idea of a set point for PWB was introduced – essentially this suggests that people have a fairly stable set point for their level of PWB and although events can lead to increases or decreases that last for a while, there is a tendency for people to return to their set point. It seems quite possible that the set point for any particular person might be heavily influenced by his or her personality. Weiss et al. (2008) have commented that PWB, "…is linked to personality by common genes and that personality may form an 'affective reserve' relevant to set-point maintenance and changes in set point over time" (p. 205). In their research (see also Chapter 2) Weiss and his colleagues studied nearly 1000 pairs of twins. They measured the well-being and personality of all of the twins and then used the statistical methods of kinship research to explore the role of genetic influences on well-being. Their results showed that there were no genetic influences directly on well-being. In particular they found that the genetic variance that underlies differences in well-being also underlies differences in personality, in particular, extraversion and neuroticism. These results support the idea that genes do not have a direct effect on happiness – but that they

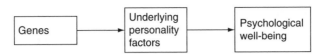

FIGURE 6.2   **Genes and personality**

influence personality – and in turn personality influences happiness (see Figure 6.2).

As explained in Chapter 4, although there is pressure to return to the set point for PWB, sometimes a permanent shift in the level of PWB does take place. As Weiss and his colleagues point out their results suggest that underlying personality might be very important in determining the speed of return to the set point, or the extent to which there is lasting change in the level of PWB.

PERSONALITY, PWB AND WORK

So, we know that personality plays an important role in determining PWB – does that mean that anyone's level of PWB at work is more dependent on their personality than situational factors, such as management, supervision, communication or resources? In fact, it is not person or situation alone that explains most of the variation in PWB. Generally both are important and it is the *interaction* between the two that has the biggest part to play. For example, someone who is creative but not very conscientious or organized may well be comfortable in a work environment where there are few firm procedures to follow but the same person would find it difficult to be happy in a work setting where systematic planning and high levels of organization were required (see Figure 6.3).

What this means is that someone's level of PWB at work is the result of three main influences. First, common sense (and the results of relevant research) tells us that the situational factors, such as the way someone is managed, do have an impact on PWB but it is also very clear that personality has a direct impact – some people just seem to have a generally happier frame of mind than others, regardless of what happens at work. And finally, most important of all is the interaction between the personality of the individual and the situation (see Figure 6.4).

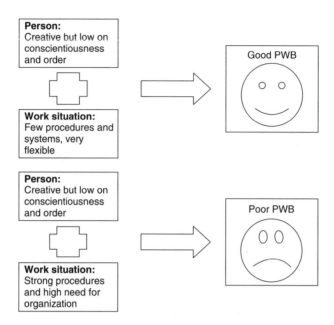

FIGURE 6.3 **Interactions between personality and situations**

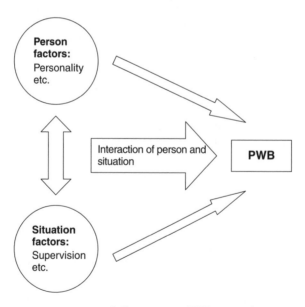

FIGURE 6.4 **Influences on PWB at work**

NON-WORK FACTORS AND PWB

It seems reasonable to expect that the main situational influences on people's PWB at work will come from factors in the workplace. The way that people are managed, the resources available, the behavior of their co-workers and several other workplace factors are all self-evidently important influences on anyone's PWB at work. Although factors in the workplace are, in general, likely to have the biggest impact on levels of PWB it is also clear that things that happen outside work can have a carryover effect to the workplace. Someone with a sick child at home, someone who has recently been burgled or involved in a serious road traffic accident will be very unlikely to be able to com-pletely forget about these things as soon as he or she arrives at work. The main non-work factors that are important for PWB at work relate to individual health factors and social and domestic factors. Physical health and psychological health are intimately related and as research reviewed in other chapters of this book has shown, damage to PWB at work can lead to both major and minor physical health problems. These effects also work the other way round – with health problems that are unrelated to work having an effect on PWB in the workplace. There is very little research evidence about the impact that physical illness has on PWB at work but it is obvious that the lowering of PWB associated with illness is likely to be a generalized effect and will have an impact on how people feel at work, especially with more serious illnesses. As well as possibly affecting PWB at work, physical ill-nesses are likely to have two major types of impact: presenteeism and absenteeism.

Presenteeism occurs when people are at work but not fully healthy. Turning up to work when sick seems likely to lead to a number of problems for both the employee and the employer. From the employ-ees' perspective working when sick may lead to longer-term problems. High-profile examples of this kind of thing include examples of sports players who play, with the aid of pain-killing injections, when they are carrying injuries. The long-term consequences of this can be seri-ous and there are many ex-professional players with severe mobility problems probably caused by playing through injury. In more seden-tary workplaces the illness problems and long-term consequences of presenteeism are different but may be just as severe. There seems to be quite a lot of confusion about the issue of presenteeism, in terms of both what it actually is and the costs and other problems associated with it. Chapter 2 provides more information on the prevalence of presenteeism and related costs.

Although with some illnesses, including psychological problems, it is feasible for people to continue working, it is often the case that illness leads to a period of sickness-absence from work. When the illness is relatively minor this period of sickness-absence is likely to be short and re-entering work will probably be fairly straightforward. For longer-term sickness-absence the problems of re-entering the workplace, or even of returning to work at all, can become much more serious. When considering the return to work of someone who has been away sick for a long period there are certain key principles that can be helpful. Some of the most important considerations are given in Table 6.2.

As Table 6.2 suggests it is likely to be much better for the individual to be at work, rather than away from work. Work provides people with structure, goals, opportunities to achieve something, contact with other people and a range of other psychologically important benefits. Research has confirmed the positive benefits of working – see Waddell and Burton (2006) – "Is work good for your health and well-being?" The consequences of being out of work are damaging and can be extreme – for example suicide (Lundin and Tomas, 2009) – but also include a range of negative consequences for both physical and psychological health. Frances McKee-Ryan and colleagues (McKee-Ryan et al., 2005) analyzed the results of over 100 studies looking at the impact of unemployment and found links between unemployment and both physical and mental health outcomes. Their results showed that unemployed people had lower levels of well-being than employed people – and that as people move from employment into

TABLE 6.2   **Returning to work after sickness-absence**

Key considerations in successful return to work

✓ Being at work is generally better for people of working age than being workless
✓ A full-time return to work is not necessarily the best first step
✓ A direct return to the normal workplace, rather than supported employment or prevocational training is more successful
✓ Line managers need to be briefed and involved
✓ Adjustments to the nature and intensity of the work may be required, especially in the short term

---

unemployment their well-being deteriorates. They also found that the process of searching for jobs, although it increases the probability of re-employment, is associated with a decrease in well-being – probably because of the inevitable frustration and feelings of rejection if a suitable job is not found quickly. In many cases it may be better for someone to return to work from long-term sickness-absence in a staged way, where both the hours worked and the nature and intensity of the work done are gradually built up to previous levels. Although a return to full-time work may not be the best first step, recent research strongly suggests that a return to the real workplace, rather than supported employment or similar is most effective, especially for people with mental health problems (Perkins et al., 2009).

SOCIAL AND DOMESTIC FACTORS

Everyone, except the most extreme workaholic, has a life outside work and from time to time, for everyone, balancing the demands of work and non-work can be tricky. Although the competing demands of work and social/domestic factors can cause problems, it is important to recognize that what people do outside work can also have a beneficial effect and help people to cope with the demands of work. The potential for positive interaction between work and out of work activities seems to be a very important factor in people's overall PWB – and hence their PWB at work. There are several ways in which the roles that people have at work and their out of work activities can interact in a positive or negative fashion (see Table 6.3).

TABLE 6.3 **Interactions between work and outside work**

Positive	Negative
☑ Work and outside factors combine positively to increase overall well-being	☒ Work and non-work factors conflict and have a negative impact on PWB
☑ Stress in one area (e.g. work) is buffered by the positive impact of the other area	☒ Negative experiences from one area spill over and have a negative impact on the other
☑ Positive experiences and resources gathered in one role can spill over positively to another	☒ The depletion of resources due to stress in one have a negative impact on the other

One important factor in maintaining good levels of personal resilience (people's ability to cope with high pressure and adversity) is to take sufficient periods of respite, especially when working intensely over a long period. Respite does not have to take the form of physical relaxation – what seems most important is that the respite provides a break from work and something that is different. The pursuit of interests outside work can provide important benefits. Research has shown (Winwood et al., 2007) that people with higher levels of activity (exercise, creative activities, social activities and so on) appear to cope more effectively with the strain of work and recover better from work-induced fatigue, sleep better and report generally lower levels of fatigue. Other research has shown that people who report a higher quality, more satisfying family life are less affected by work-related stress.

Of course, although the research reported above suggests that out of work activity can be beneficial and help people to enjoy work more, it is also the case that, some of the time, demands from outside work make working life more difficult, rather than easier. One of the key positive functions of time away from work is to provide an opportunity for recovery. Without the opportunity to recover, for example in the evening at the end of the working day, people will rapidly become exhausted and both psychological and physical health problems will follow. For people who work in more stressful roles and work more intensively recovery periods are particularly important. There is evidence to show that the more intensive the working day, the longer it takes people to unwind after work (e.g. Meijman et al., 1992). It is also true that jobs that make higher demands seem to create a stronger need for recovery (Sonnentag and Zjistra, 2006). When there is too little respite for the recovery process to complete before work is resumed, there will be an increase in fatigue and consequent loss of performance and likely knock-on health consequences. Outside work activities and demands can start to have a negative impact when they interfere with the respite process. The demands placed on working people by certain types of circumstances have been shown to have a negative impact on health and well-being. The strains imposed on dual career couples, caregivers, single parents, frequent (work-related) travel, shift work and irregular working routines have all been associated with damage to well-being.

Essentially the issues in the area of work/non-work revolve around a number of key factors. First as already explained, when non-work provides respite. This will build resources and have a positive impact on

	Manageable work demands	Resilient and able to cope with challenge and new demands	Vulnerable May be susceptible to negative spill over from non-work
Work			
	High-intensity work demands of significant duration	Vulnerable but maybe OK Possible positive spill over	At risk! – cause for concern and unlikely to be sustainable
		Likely to provide respite and support *	**May interfere with respite and recovery or conflict with work demands** **

FIGURE 6.5 **Work and non-work**

Note: * For example, positive social/family life, leisure pursuits that enhance respite and do not conflict with work.
** For example, caregiving duties, frequent travel, poor family relationships, chronic illness and so on.

PWB. When the non-work situation is such that respite may be inter-fered with, rather than enhanced, this will lead to problems. Of course not all dual career couples or caregivers have problems but the research suggests that people in certain situations need to be particularly careful to ensure respite and a balance between the demands of work and non-work. A second key point concerns the intensity and duration of work demands. At times when work demands are high the potential benefits of non-work become more important and need to be protected. A third point concerns the quality of family and other non-work relationships. When these are good, they appear to exert a moderating effect on the impact of workplace strain – when they are poor, the opposite is true.

For any individual or anyone responsible for managing the well-being of others, Figure 6.5 gives an indication of likely levels of vulnerability and resilience. Clearly the major indicator of potential concern is when someone is working at a high intensity in a situation where there are factors that are known to be linked to risks to well-being.

CHAPTER 7

WORK AND WELL-BEING

As Chapter 6 explained, PWB at work is influenced by many factors that are not directly work-related. These factors are important and it is crucial to recognize that what goes on at work is not the only thing that influences PWB at work. It is equally important to recognize that what actually goes on at work is generally the most important factor in how people feel at work. Work-related factors are the most important contributors to PWB at work partly because they have a direct impact on PWB but also because it is easier for organizations to change and improve work-related factors. Improving someone's relationships with members of their family is not something that an organization might normally expect to be able to do – but improving relationships with someone's manager or colleagues is a different matter.

This chapter focuses on the workplace factors that are likely to have most impact on PWB at work. The key factors that have an impact on PWB may be divided into four main clusters: the work itself and its context; the work–home interface; purpose and meaning at work and leadership, management and supervision. Table 7.1 gives a brief overview of these clusters.

This chapter discusses each cluster in turn and then shows how they can be used to provide an overall model of how workplace factors and PWB combine to produce the important organizational outcomes reviewed in Chapter 2.

WORK AND ITS CONTEXT

The actual work that people do has an important influence on levels of PWB at work. In many ways it is obvious that the nature of the work itself will have an impact on someone's PWB. But what is it about work that is important for PWB? Ask anyone about what

78

TABLE 7.1 **Four main clusters of workplace factors important for PWB**

Cluster	Examples from clusters
Work and its context	■ Work demands ■ Access to resources and equipment ■ Effectiveness of communication in the organization
Relationships at work and the work–home interface	■ Relationships with colleagues ■ Social support
Purpose and meaning	■ Clarity about work goals ■ Feeling that work goals are worthwhile
Leadership, management and supervision	■ Impact that manager has on the workgroup ■ Leadership commitment to employee PWB

makes a good job and you will get a range of answers. Perhaps the first thing that comes to mind for most people, when thinking about the desirability of different types of work, is pay. In itself pay seems to be unrelated to happiness and well-being once a certain threshold is passed. Several studies have shown that for individuals and even for whole national groups pay does not bring happiness. Of course, pay and rewards matter to people but beyond a certain level of reward what seems to become important is the extent to which people feel that they are being fairly rewarded, especially in comparison to others. In absolute terms pay, just like other rewards or achievements, may have only a transient effect (see the ideas of set point and the "hedonic treadmill" in Chapter 4).

Pay is important and clearly central to why people go to work but it is not an integral aspect of the work itself. Further reflection on the desirable characteristics of work, going beyond those discussed so far, leads to thoughts about a range of factors such as the purpose of the job and its usefulness, the degree of freedom and autonomy available to a jobholder, the satisfaction derived from using skills to carry out the job and so on. The demands that a job makes is a good place to start when thinking about whether a specific job seems desirable or not. Most people would feel that a job that made minimal demands and required no actions or activity would be boring and not very interesting. Of course there are some people who might be happy with such a job – but for most of us some level of demand is important. For example, even if it were extremely well-paid a job involving no activity, other than watching a CCTV (on which nothing interesting or significant took place) for many hours at a stretch would not seem attractive.

Such a job would be more interesting if it also involved periodic tours of a building, or if actions were often required in response to what was seen on the CCTV – it would become even more desirable for many if it also involved working with colleagues carrying out similar roles, and/or periodically interacting with members of the public who required assistance. For many people nowadays, the idea of working in a call center provides a powerful example of the type of work that is undesirable and probably psychologically unhealthy. Indeed there is evidence that the work in some call centers does have quite negative consequences for staff who work there, including high levels of stress and employee turnover (see Holdsworth and Cartwright, 2003) and physical health consequences such as weight gain (Boyce et al., 2008). In practice of course, all call centers are not the same and although some may be depressing and uninteresting places to work, some are not like this. Some of the problems associated with call centers, including the lack of control experienced due to electronic monitoring and the excessive quantitative monitoring of performance, may be overcome by undertaking initiatives designed to provide operatives with more control – and also to make the work more satisfying and meaningful – for example, including a "quality" aspect to performance monitoring in addition to quantitative assessment of indicators such as call length. These examples of the pros and cons of different types of work illustrate many of the key factors that seem to be important in determining whether work is psychologically healthy and desirable.

Early research on the design of work focused on a number of factors that were found to be linked to the satisfaction (or dissatisfaction) that people derived from their work. Following on from the pioneering work of people like Fred Herzberg, who focused on what makes work satisfying, researchers began to conduct empirical studies in the workplace that started to pin down some of the key factors. Richard Hackman and Greg Oldham developed a particularly influential model called the "Job Characteristics Model". This model identified five core job characteristics. These characteristic were:

Skill variety: the extent to which the job requires a range of skills;
Task significance: the extent to which the job has an impact on others, either within or outside the organization;
Task identity: the extent to which the job produces a whole, identifiable outcome;

Autonomy: the extent to which the job allows the jobholder to exercise choice and discretion in his or her work; and

Feedback from job: the extent to which the job itself provides information on how well the jobholder is doing (it's important to note that this refers to feedback that is part of the job itself, rather than feedback from others).

According to the model, these job characteristics have an impact on people's psychological state, which in turn influence their motivation, satisfaction and work performance.

Until the development of models such as the Job Characteristics Model, the primary driver behind the design of work had been to design it to maximize efficiency and performance. The development of models such as this – together with the associated research support for the underlying ideas – caused a huge shift in emphasis. Essentially the emphasis moved away from a focus on performance and efficiency toward recognition of the importance of considering the feelings, satisfaction and motivation of the jobholder when designing work. There are many well-known examples of job design initiatives, such as the work done at Volvo's Torslanda plant to introduce job rotation and then semi-autonomous workgroups, or Texas Instruments' moves to redesign the jobs of cleaners and janitors (see Robertson and Smith, 1985).

As mentioned in Chapter 2 of this book, the key aspects of jobs that are linked to the PWB of the jobholder revolve around the four core concepts of *demands, control, support and sense of purpose and meaning*. In essence jobs that promote and sustain the well-being of the jobholders need to provide a good balance for these key factors. As already noted, a job that makes too few demands will not be satisfying. The demands of a job provide the jobholder with an opportunity to achieve – and the positive feelings associated with achievement are important for PWB. Allowing people an appropriate degree of control is also psychologically healthy. Denying people control produces the type of situation outlined above in poorly designed call center work, where operatives have their behavior constrained and controlled unduly. On the other hand, abandoning an inexperienced operative and just leaving them to get on with it takes the idea of control and empowerment too far! The support and resources available to people also have an impact. A very demanding role in which support, control and resources are plentiful may still be very satisfying and psychologically healthy. In one way or another all of these factors combine and interact to provide a degree of pressure on the jobholder.

POSITIVE PRESSURE

One of the most constructive ways of looking at the pressures that are created by jobs is to classify pressure into two categories: challenge pressures and hindrance pressures. Challenge pressures are generally seen as positive and although they may create a degree of strain for the jobholder they are psychologically healthy. Challenge pressures are associated with factors that promote growth and development and provide individuals with an opportunity to achieve. By contrast, hindrance pressures create barriers to achievement, growth and accomplishment at work. Some examples of challenge and hindrance pressures are given in Table 7.2.

The distinction is important because the different types of pressure have very different consequences for jobholders. Hindrance pressures are likely to damage performance and in the longer run they will almost certainly chip away at an individual's reservoir of PWB. Nathan Podsakoff and his colleagues (Podsakoff et al., 2007) took a systematic look at the impact that challenge and hindrance pressures have on some important organizational variables, such as job satisfaction and employee turnover. They identified a large number of

TABLE 7.2 **Examples of challenge and hindrance pressures**

■ **Hindrance pressures**
Role ambiguity
Poor work relationships
Job insecurity
Lack of control
Unclear goals
Unrealistic deadlines

■ **Challenge pressures**
Workload
Additional responsibility (with appropriate training and support)
Time pressure
Job scope
Goals that are seen as worthwhile
Tight deadlines

studies (over 150 independent samples in total) in which relationships between challenge/hindrance pressures and employee turnover and satisfaction had been studied. They then used meta-analysis statistical techniques to summarize the findings. Challenge stressors included things like pressure to complete tasks, time urgency and workloads. Hindrance stressors included measures of situational constraints, hassles, organizational politics, resource inadequacies, role ambiguity, role conflict and role overload. Some of their results are summarized in Table 7.3.

The results in Table 7.3 show the correlations between challenge and hindrance pressures and the various outcomes. The size of the correlation (between 0 and 1) indicates how strongly the two variables are related. The direction of the correlation (+ or −) indicates whether the two factors vary positively together (+ve) or as one increases the other decreases (−ve). The most striking finding in the table is the strong negative association between job satisfaction and hindrance pressures, illustrating the powerful link between hindrance pressures and job dissatisfaction. By contrast, challenge pressures are positively linked to satisfaction and commitment. Hindrance pressures also show sizeable relationships with turnover and intention to leave. One final point worth emphasizing is the positive relationship between strain and both types of pressure. In other words, both challenge and hindrance pressure lead to strain. This raises an important point about the relationship between pressure and well-being. Sometimes people form the mistaken impression that developing PWB at work is about ensuring that people never feel under pressure. This is wrong! The misunderstanding is often based on confusion between pressure, strain and stress. As the results above suggest, some degree of challenge is an important ingredient in a job – and clearly challenge brings with it a degree of pressure – and quite probably the jobholder will experience some degree of strain. This is not necessarily a problem and

TABLE 7.3 **Correlations between types of pressure and outcomes**

Type of Pressure	Strain	Job satisfaction	Commitment	Turnover	Withdrawal
Hindrance	+0.56	−0.57	−0.52	+0.23	+0.22
Challenge	+0.40	+0.02	+0.04	−0.04	−0.07

Podsakoff et al., Jour Appl Psych, 2007.
Source: Podsakoff et al. (2007).

may quite possibly be healthy. If the balance of demands, resources support and control are such that the jobholder can deal with the pressure and achieve worthwhile goals, then all is well. The jobholder has the opportunity to achieve and develop and benefit from the positive psychological experiences that go along with achieving valued results. If, for some reason (e.g. lack of support), the demands exceed the jobholder's ability to cope, then problems arise and the pressures are likely to lead to stress, defined by the Health and Safety Executive in the United Kingdom as, "The adverse reaction people have to excessive pressures or other types of demand placed on them at work" (http://www.hse.gov.uk/stress/furtheradvice/whatisstress.htm).

Note the use of the term "excessive" in relation to pressure – it's only a problem when pressure becomes excessive.

In real work settings the classification of pressures into either challenge or hindrance may well depend on other factors. For example, an increase in responsibility and workload may be challenging if it is coupled with appropriate support and training but if not it may be seen as a hindrance – and damage both performance and well-being. The pressure–performance curve in Figure 7.1 summarizes the way in which pressure relates to performance and PWB.

In Figure 7.1 the "feel-good zone" is where someone carrying out a job in which challenge, support, demands and control are in balance

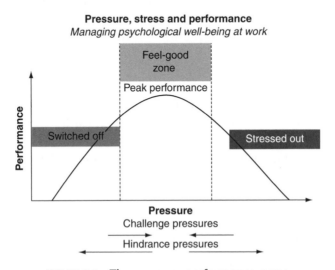

FIGURE 7.1 **The pressure–performance curve**

and creating positive pressure. In general, challenge pressures will push the jobholder toward the center of the curve where both performance and well-being are high. By contrast, hindrance pressures exert outward pressure, leading to low performance and either stress and burnout or switching off (low engagement).

These key principles raise the important question of how to manage pressure at work – and how to ensure positive pressure. Part of the solution is to ensure that the key features of jobs themselves are designed to maximize the important job characteristics that are linked to PWB and performance. But although the design of the work is very important, especially for more routine positions, the other three factors introduced at the beginning of this chapter (work relationships and the work–home interface; purpose and meaning at work; and leadership, management and supervision) must also be considered.

RELATIONSHIPS AT WORK AND THE WORK–HOME INTERFACE

As the section above demonstrates, the actual work that people do can have an important impact on PWB. For almost everyone, being at work involves some level of interaction with other people. The quality of these interactions and the extent to which they are supportive and rewarding is an important ingredient in how people feel at work. Positive relationships with others can play a part in helping people to cope with the demands of a job. For many people one of the most enjoyable aspects of the work is the contact it provides with others. Also, when there are difficulties at work or even at home many people find their immediate colleagues to be a good source of support. It is also clear from research on the consequences of unemployment that one of the important roles that a job plays in the lives of employed people is to provide a source of social interaction. On the negative side, there is sometimes a demand for people to engage in significant "emotional labor" while they are at work. Emotional labor refers to "the effort, planning, and control needed to express organizationally desired emotions during interpersonal transactions" (Morris and Feldman, 1996, p. 98). For example, a nurse dealing with a very difficult patient may need to engage in significant emotional labor to retain composure and not display signs of anger or irritation. There are many types of job that involve significant levels of emotional labor on a daily basis because of the customers/clients/patients that the jobholder needs to deal with. For others the emotional labor may be required to deal with colleagues or other co-workers. In any case there is often a require-ment for people to regulate the expression of their emotions. This can involve not expressing an emotion that we experience, for example not showing frustration or anger with someone who is obstructing progress. Emotional labor may also involve expressing an emotion that we do not feel – smiling and appearing happy when we feel low. If the requirements to monitor and regulate emotions go unchecked, they may eventually result in emotional exhaustion and burnout (Mann, 1999; Grandey, 2000; Lewig and Dollard, 2003). It may be that a requirement to display certain emotions at work is not in itself prob-lematic. The negative issues arise when the requirement to display or control emotion is not congruent with the emotion that is being experienced.

In addition to the challenge and support provided by relationships with others in the workplace, there is also the impact that factors out-side work can have on PWB at work. As explained in Chapter 6, there is potential for factors outside work to have a positive or negative spillover effect on PWB at work. Also out of work factors may create conflicting time demands and have a negative impact on workplace levels of PWB. One aspect of importance to the home–work interface that was not discussed in Chapter 6 relates to the patterns of work (e.g. shift work) that a jobholder follows. One very straightforward fac-tor here concerns the impact on well-being of the actual number of hours worked. There is some evidence that working long hours can have a negative impact on health and well-being. For example, Van der Hulst (2003) found links between long hours and physical health fac-tors such as cardiovascular disease, and other studies (e.g. Sparks et al., 1997; Kirkaldy et al., 2000) have found links with long hours and poor psychological health. Working for more than 48 hours per week may be a key trigger point but the findings are not entirely straightforward. Other factors such as the opportunities for respite and rest breaks, the type of work and the extent to which the hours worked are voluntary or involuntary may determine whether the long hours have a detri-mental impact on health and well-being or not. As well as the absolute number of hours worked, other factors related to work patterns may also have an impact on health and well-being; these include working full-time versus part-time, shift work and time spent traveling to and from work.

FLEXIBLE WORKING

One key working practice that seems to have a positive impact on PWB is flexibility. Initially the introduction of flexible working arrangements was often about being family friendly, in particular, helping women return to work or to balance the demands of work and family. However, employee demand has led to a change in emphasis and a move away from family friendly terminology. Providing adequate work–life balance is becoming a central part of human resource strategy and employee relations in the twenty-first century and flexible working arrangements provide a useful tool to achieve the goal of good work–life balance. For many organizations operating in a 24/7 mode requires a different relationship with their workforce and is another driver toward flexible working practices. In many countries government has also seen the need to integrate work and life outside work and started to encourage organizations to consider the business case for flexible working practices.

In essence flexible working practices involve providing employees with flexibility about when they work, where they work – or both of these. There are many different types of flexible working schemes. Some of the main ones are described in Table 7.4.

Although, in principle, the introduction of flexible working arrangements sounds straightforward, the potential benefits are not automatic and there are many considerations involved in their successful implementation. By and large, when flexible working is introduced in an organization it should be offered to as many members of staff as possible. This avoids the difficulties that are sometimes reported when members of staff who are not allowed to work flexibly feel that they are put under additional pressure because of the flexible working of others. A clear policy and equitable implementation by management is also important – denying one member of a team flexible working but allowing it for another who does the same job may cause difficulties. The judgment about whether an individual will benefit from flexible working is best left to the individual himself or herself, regardless of whether or not they appear to have a "need" for flexible working arrangement (e.g. small children at home or elderly relatives to care for). See Lewis (2003) for a review of research relating to flexible working practices.

TABLE 7.4 **Some flexible working arrangements**

Flexible working arrangement	Brief description
Flexitime	Employees have a set "core" period when they are expected to be at the place of work but outside the core they can start and finish at their own discretion
Home-working	Working from home, some or all of the time
Compressed working week	Compressing a full week's work (e.g. 40 hours) into 4 days – or a 9-day fortnight
Annualized hours	The number of hours an employee is required to work is calculated over the whole year
Term time working	When an employee works only during school term times
Reduced hours	Usually for a set period (e.g. 3 months) an employee has an agreement to work fewer hours
Job sharing	A full-time job is divided between, say, two people. Each person works different hours and has his or her own separate contract of employment
Career break	Not working for an agreed period of time – and returning to work with the same level of seniority as before the break

In many countries, including most of Europe and the United States flexible working has shown a steady increase over the last decade or so (Great Place to Work, 2004; Hooker et al., 2006). In a survey conducted in the United Kingdom, for example, over 90 percent of employees felt that at least one form of flexible working would be available to them if required. From an employee's perspective, the most popular form of flexible working seems to be flexitime, with nearly half of UK employees who had flexitime available to them making use of it (Hooker et al., 2006). Generally employees seem to feel positively about flexible working practices. Research into the benefits of flexible working suggests that they are likely to depend on several factors, which include the type of flexible working arrangement and the circumstances of the individual employee. There is some indication that flexibility about the timing of work (e.g. flexitime) is more beneficial for reducing work–family conflicts. Studies evaluating the benefits to work–family conflict have produced positive results for flexible schedules of work

(Byron, 2005) but not for flexibility more generally (Mesmer-Magnus and Viswesvaran, 2006).

SENSE OF PURPOSE AND MEANING

It should already be clear from other material in this book (see Chapters 1 and 4 in particular) that PWB is not just about feeling good and doing things that are relaxing. To be psychologically healthy we need to feel that what we are doing is worthwhile and serves a useful purpose. The purpose may be extremely altruistic and involve serving or helping others – or it may be more selfish and be focused on improving our own station in life. The fact that high PWB is not based on relaxing and drifting around as we please has very important implications for the workplace. Most importantly, it means that the work people do needs to have some reasonable degree of challenge associated with it – and it needs to feel worthwhile. There is proof of this from many different psychological studies and the principle that people need to feel that what they are doing (at work) is worthwhile is embodied in many theories about well-being, work performance and motivation. For example, the most successful motivational theory is the theory of goal-setting developed by Edwin Locke and Gary Latham (see Locke and Latham, 2002; Locke and Latham, 2009). This approach is based on the premise that goals will affect actions – and a large research literature has shown how the setting of goals that are specific, difficult but achievable leads to high levels of performance. But there is an important caveat – goals will affect performance much more effectively when the individual is committed to the goals. Other approaches, more directly related to the nature of the work that people do, such as the Job Characteristics Model (see earlier in this chapter), emphasize that to be satisfying and motivating jobs need to be meaningful for the jobholder – and lead to outcomes that are important for them and others. In brief, people need to feel committed to what they do at work and that it is meaningful and worthwhile. All of this can be summarized by saying that people need to have a clear "Sense of Purpose".

Obviously the type of goals that people have and how worthwhile these seem will have a big part to play in the sense of purpose at work that people experience. In turn the role of management and leadership is extremely important in creating a clear sense of purpose and work goals that seem worthwhile.

MANAGEMENT AND LEADERSHIP

Almost all of the literature and guidance that is focused on PWB at work places a great deal of emphasis on the role of managers. For example, the primary approach of the British Health and Safety Executive (HSE) for tackling work-related stress focuses on a set of "management standards" (see Table 7.5). In collaboration with the Chartered Institute for Personnel and Development the HSE have also commissioned research and development work to identify the management competencies that are required for managers to successfully implement the management standards (Yarker et al., 2008).

Other important reports dealing with PWB at work, such as the UK government's Foresight Mental capital and Wellbeing Project (2008), also emphasize the role that line managers play in determining PWB at work. This heavy emphasis on line managers is based on research that shows the impact that management has on people's well-being at work. The quality of exchanges between employees and their boss has been shown to be an important predictor of whether people leave

TABLE 7.5 **The Health and Safety Executive's management standards***
approach

The Management Standards cover six key areas of work design that, if not properly managed, are associated with poor health and well-being, lower productivity and increased-sickness-absence. In other words, the six Management Standards cover the primary sources of stress at work. These are:

- Demands – this includes issues such as workload, work patterns and the work environment.
- Control – how much say the person has in the way they do their work.
- Support – this includes the encouragement, sponsorship and resources provided by the organization, line management and colleagues.
- Relationships – this includes promoting positive working to avoid conflict and dealing with unacceptable behavior.
- Role – whether people understand their role within the organization and whether the organization ensures that they do not have conflicting roles.
- Change – how organizational change (large or small) is managed and communicated in the organization.

The Management Standards represent a set of conditions that, if present, reflects a high level of health well-being and organizational performance.

Note: * Reproduced with permission.

or stay in an organization (Griffeth et al., 2000). But the relationship between an employee and his or her manager is not only linked to employee turnover, but it is also linked closely to the PWB of employees. In some respects it is quite easy to see how the manager might have a major impact on the PWB of employees. The manager is (or should be) closely involved in setting the goals for an employee. The manager can also exert a significant impact on the kind of factors identified by HSE and others as important determinants of PWB at work. For example, the level of control and autonomy that an employee experiences could be seriously limited by a manager who tries to micro-manage all of his or her employees' tasks. The demands placed on people, the resources and support available together with levels of work–life balance can all be influenced by the manager. Of course, the manager is not always in full control of all of these factors – but he or she can certainly have some impact. Levels of control, workload, support and so on will also be constrained by the nature of the work and how it is designed and many wider organizational and cultural factors. In some cases line managers themselves may find life difficult because they do NOT have the authority to influence key factors that they know are damaging for their workforce! See Gilbreath (2004) for further information on research studies looking at the impact of managers on critical factors that determine PWB, such as role ambiguity or conflict, task autonomy, the balance between job demands and control. There is also a substantial amount of research showing how supervisory or leadership style links to perceived stress, strain and burnout in subordinates (e.g. Sosik and Godshalk, 2000). Poor quality exchanges between the manager and his or her direct reports have been linked to higher perceived stress (Nelson et al., 1998). There has also been research linking supervisor and leadership approaches with employee health complaints (Landeweerd and Boumans, 1994) and with burnout (Martin and Schinke, 1998). It also seems that the behavior of managers can have an influence on how well people deal with some of the types of "hindrance" pressures (see earlier in this chapter) such as lack of resources and day-to-day hassles (Snelgrove and Phil, 2001).

Flint-Taylor and Robertson (2007; Robertson and Flint-Taylor, 2009) in their Leadership Impact model have proposed that the core issue for a manager in maintaining employee PWB revolves around the extent to which the employee is challenged and/or supported. As explained earlier in this chapter, challenge pressures are positive and being able to reach challenging goals is a critical factor in building PWB, enabling people to experience achievement, mastery and to build self-confidence. It seems important that leaders avoid what Kaplan (2006) refers to as "lopsidedness", when they are either not challenging enough, and let people off the hook, or not supportive enough and hold people strictly accountable in an overbearing and eventually demoralizing fashion.

Good quality leadership and management can have a very positive impact on PWB. Gilbreath and Benson (2004) looked at the impact of managers' behavior on PWB. What they found was that supervisor behavior contributed to the prediction of psychiatric disturbance over and above the impact of other factors including age, health practices, support from other people at work, support from home, stressful life events and stressful work events. As they noted, "...this provides additional evidence that supervisor behaviour can affect employee well-being and suggests that those seeking to create healthier workplaces should not neglect supervision" (Gilbreath and Benson, 2004, p. 255). Managers who develop high-quality work practices within their workgroups can have a positive impact on well-being (see also Alimo-Metcalfe et al., 2008). Interestingly, the well-being of a workgroup also has a reciprocal effect on the well-being of the leader (Van Dierendonck et al., 2004), so those who nurture the well-being of their workgroups through high-quality leadership practices also get a beneficial impact, in the longer term, on their own well-being! How leaders and managers can most effectively develop the well-being of their workgroups is explained in Chapter 9.

Earlier chapters in this book have demonstrated the positive impact that high PWB can have for organizations, for individual employees – and now we can see that there are also benefits for managers who have a positive impact on the well-being of their workgroup. This is a win-win-win situation – are there many other aspects of working life that can lead to such positive outcomes for all concerned?

PART 4

GETTING THE BENEFITS

CHAPTER 8

IMPROVING PSYCHOLOGICAL WELL-BEING – PERSONAL DEVELOPMENT AND RESILIENCE

Two people can be working in very similar situations, with equally similar personal and family circumstances, yet one seems to be positive, resilient and psychologically healthy, the other doesn't. How can this be and what does it imply? Essentially, this can happen because there are two main sets of factors that exert an influence on people's PWB. The first set of factors relates to the situation – especially the work situation. Much of the material in this book has concentrated on the impact that these situational factors (management, type of work, access to resources, levels of control and autonomy, personal circumstances etc.) can have on PWB. There is no doubt that "situation" factors can have a major impact on PWB but it is very important to recognize that the impact of the situation on PWB can be significantly moderated by "person" factors – qualities such as optimism, resilience or positive thinking that are related to the individual himself or herself. These "person" factors help to explain the differences in PWB experienced by two people who are working in essentially the same situation (see Figure 8.1).

Earlier chapters (4 and 6) have explained how certain underlying personality factors are related to people's levels of PWB. Personality factors reflect the relatively fixed and stable "person" factors. This chapter takes a more dynamic perspective and moves on from the links between relatively stable personality factors and PWB to explore what can be done to protect and enhance PWB through "person" factors that can be changed and developed. As explained in Chapter 6, the two main personality traits associated with PWB are extraversion and

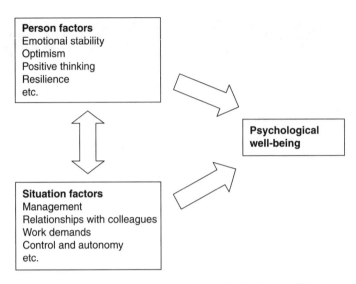

FIGURE 8.1   **Person, situation and psychological well-being**

neuroticism. Personality traits do play a significant role in determining a wide range of the feelings, emotions and ways of thinking that are important for PWB. Personality factors are important because they determine people's tendency (predisposition) to specific psychological experiences or behaviors. For example, as explained in Chapter 6, people who are more neurotic have a stronger predisposition to experience negative emotions and to feel anxious. But it is important to remember that although personality controls predispositions to psychological experiences or tendencies to behave in certain ways, it does not directly determine how we behave or feel. This is a very important point because, in everyday language, what it means is that while personality may be largely stable and is not easily changed, the same is not true of our behavior and ways of thinking.

RESILIENCE

Let's now build on the example given at the beginning of this chapter – where two people with very similar situational influences have observably different levels of PWB. Since the situation is the same – it must be person factors that are responsible for the differences. So, what are the most important differences between someone who is able to retain resilience, optimism and PWB and someone who isn't? Obviously we may expect to see personality differences between the two people, since we already know that personality is related to the levels of PWB that people experience – and also to the typical "set point" (see Chapter 4) that people have for their level of PWB. It is very likely, however, that personality alone will not explain the main difference between two such individuals. This might be especially true if one of them has undertaken some skills-based or personal development, such as resilience training, to help protect and build their PWB. People who are resilient are better able to retain their PWB even in difficult situations. The research in this area reveals that there are certain key behaviors and ways of thinking that go along with higher levels of resilience. Although underlying personality represents the starting point for any individual's level of resilience, there is much that can be done, regardless of this starting point, to develop better resilience and to protect and enhance PWB. There are two very important points to understand about personal resilience. The first concerns the starting point, which is determined to a very large extent by underlying personality. The second point is that resilience is best thought of as a combination of qualities, rather than as a single quality that people have or lack. Considering an example may help to make both of these points clear.

To understand a person's personality properly, it would be necessary to look at the more detailed facet level scores for each of the five factors but for this illustration it is OK to look at the overall "Big Five" level. Chris is someone who is very conscientious and quite extraverted, whereas Mel is quite introverted and not very conscientious. Both Mel and Chris are quite neurotic. With these personality profiles they would be likely to thrive in very different work situations. If Mel was working in a role that demanded precision, a high level of organization and the need to initiate contact with previously unknown people, this would be extremely challenging. Mel's anxiety might become a problem and an observer might feel that Mel was not very resilient. Chris would probably find this type of role easier to cope with but would almost certainly seem less resilient in a role that required free flowing thinking, a great deal of flexibility and solitary work – something that Mel might take to quite well.

In many ways, the process of developing resilience is about building on the foundation provided by our underlying personality to help us cope with situations and challenges that we may initially (because

TABLE 8.1 **A resilience prescription**

- Focus on positive emotions and an optimistic thinking style
- Develop cognitive flexibility – learn to "reframe"
- Develop coping strategies – make active use of them and face fears
- Take on challenges to enable yourself to experience mastery
- Recognize and develop signature strengths
- Find a resilient role model – actively finding one is important
- Personal moral compass – sense of purpose
- Establish and nurture a supportive social network
- Look after your physical condition – exercise may be the "magic bullet"

of our underlying personality) find difficult. The general requirements for resilience are fairly standard (see below) but, depending on their underlying personality, people will develop some of the requirements naturally – and will need work to develop others. Research looking at the characteristics of people who appear to be resilient even in situations of extreme adversity has identified a range of key characteristics and behaviors – a formulation of these in a "Resilience Profile" is given in Table 8.1.

The prescription given in Table 8.1 is derived from research in a range of different areas, including psycho-biology (e.g. Haglund et al., 2007), sports and exercise psychology (e.g. Jones et al., 2002), stress management and personality (e.g. Maddi and Khobasha, 2005) and physiological psychology (e.g. Dienstbier, 1989).

POSITIVE ATTITUDES AND EMOTIONS

Developing positive attitudes and emotions is not done by some of the rather silly things that have become associated with being positive such as looking in the bathroom mirror each morning and telling yourself you're going to have a great day! This might not do any harm but such approaches lack the depth and scientific support to provide any real benefit.

The importance of experiencing positive emotions for PWB has been explored in some detail elsewhere in this book (see Chapter 4), as has the beneficial broadening and building effect that positive emotions have. So, the first requirement for developing resilience is to try to experience a good ratio of positive to negative emotions. Some research has even suggested that there might be an ideal ratio of positive versus negative emotions. Barbara Fredrickson and Marcial Losada (2005) report results suggesting that for individuals and teams the optimum levels of positive:negative emotions for high PWB is above about 3:1. In other words, better PWB is more likely when people experience over three times as many positive as negative emotions. Of course, it isn't possible to completely control the emotions that we experience but it is possible, with sufficient focus and determination, to make a difference. For example, when something bad happens at work and you start to feel low a good policy may be to try and think of something positive and use this to lighten your mood – and balance the negative feelings with something positive. Trying to think oneself into a positive emotion is not immediately an easy thing to do but something that can be achieved with practice. Barbara Fredrickson's website (http://www.positivityratio.com/single.php) enables you to take a free test and monitor your positivity ratio.

EXPLANATORY STYLE

The role of thinking in controlling emotion is absolutely critical in building resilience, maintaining positive emotions, attitudes and an overall positive frame of mind. In fact, the key to maintaining a positive frame of mind lies in how a person interprets and thinks about events. Technically this is referred to as attribution theory. One particular aspect of attribution theory, referred to as explanatory style, is particularly important for resilience, PWB and performance. Essentially explanatory style relates to whether people interpret events (particularly successes and failures) optimistically or pessimistically. Although some people may argue that a pessimistic style is useful and protective, "...if you expect bad things to happen then you won't be disappointed if they do..." the overwhelming evidence from research is that an optimistic style is much better. Before looking at some of the research evidence to support this statement let's examine what it means to use an optimistic rather than pessimistic style. The differences between pessimistic and optimistic thinking are based on three main aspects of explanatory style: internal–external; global–specific and permanent–temporary. Figure 8.2 shows the combinations that lead to pessimistic and optimistic thinking for successes and failures.

Attributional style

- Positive attributional
  style for *successes*

 – **Permanent**
  – **Internal**
  – **Global**

- Positive attributional
  style for *failures*

 – **Specific**
  – **Internal/External**
  – **Temporary**

- Negative attributional
  style for *successes*

 – **Specific**
  – **External**
  – **Temporary**

- Negative attributional
  style for *failures*

 – **Permanent**
  – **Internal**
  – **Global**

FIGURE 8.2   **Positive and negative attributional styles**

Internal–external refers to whether the causes are seen as external (other people, chance, etc.) or internal (oneself). Global–specific refers to the extent to which the attributions made are specific to a particular event (e.g. this meeting or presentation) or global (all meetings and presentations). Permanent–temporary refers to the extent to which the attributions are long-lasting (e.g. always goes wrong) or short-lived (e.g. today it went wrong). An example should help to make these points clear. As Figure 8.2 shows, when something goes badly (failure), a pessimistic style involves making attributions that are global, permanent and internal. One of the authors played a great deal of football as a younger man and at one point joined a semi-professional club. After a few games in the reserves he was selected to play for the first team – but rather than his preferred position (right back) he was positioned as left back. How did the game go? In brief, he had a real stinker! Coming off the pitch at the end of the game he felt very low. It's easy to see how a pessimistic style could worsen the bad feelings and damage resilience – I played really badly and it was my fault (internal), I'm not good enough to play at this level of football (global), I'll never make it in this club (permanent). A different set of attributions – I played badly but the manager selected me out of position and didn't give me a chance (a more external attribution – but not one that is unrealistic), I can't tell until I get a game in my correct position whether I'm good enough for this level or not (specific) and next time now that I've got some experience I might be able to perform better, even at left back (temporary). It's important to note that both sets of attributions are consistent with what happened – trying to make out that I didn't have a poor game would have been empty and unrealistic – rather

100

than authentic optimistic thinking. Thinking pessimistically about success is almost as damaging as pessimistic thinking for failures. If you deliver an excellent paper and the presentation for this goes well at an important meeting, using a pessimistic style will seriously limit the resilience building effect that a success might have – It went well but the audience was very receptive and uncritical (external); if I had been presenting on something else I would have been much shakier (specific); I got away with it this time but I was lucky and I doubt it will be so easy next time (temporary).

The baseline for positive and negative explanatory styles are dependent on personality but resilience training courses and other interventions can be very successful in helping people to develop a more positive style. The research evidence supporting the benefits of a positive explanatory style is substantial and the gains have been shown in a number of areas. One of the main areas where research has been conducted is in sales. Anyone with experience of sales jobs will recognize the extent to which a good level of personal resilience is a prerequisite. Several studies have shown that sales personnel who use a positive explanatory style outperform those who do not. Research has also shown that a positive explanatory style can be developed – and that this has an impact. In one study (Proudfoot et al., 2008) sales personnel were given attributional style training. The participants were randomly assigned to a training group or to a waiting list. The results for the trained group showed that their attributional style had changed after the training – in favor of a more positive style. The results also showed improvements in a number of other psychological variables, including PWB; furthermore employee turnover was significantly reduced and general productivity improved. The participants on the waiting list were subsequently trained, so that their pre- and post-training results could be compared with the trained group – and their results showed the same post-training improvements. Explanatory style has also been shown to be linked to success in other fields, including sporting performance (e.g. Martin-Krumm et al., 2003).

Training in explanatory style (essentially optimistic, rather than pessimistic thinking) thus has the potential to build resilience and help to support PWB and performance. In fact, there seems to be a natural tendency for people to interpret positive events by using a positive explanatory style. In an analysis of over 250 studies Amy Mezulis and colleagues (Mezulis et al., 2004) found a trend toward a "self-serving" bias – that is, making more internal, global and stable attributions (e.g.

"it went really well, I'm good at things like that") for positive events compared with negative ones. For people with psychological illness the trend was less pronounced, suggesting that they get less psychological benefit from using positive styles and interpret positive events more negatively. As Burns and Seligman (1989) suggest, negative explanatory style may be an enduring risk factor for depression, low achievement and physical illness.

FLEXIBLE THINKING

Developing a more positive explanatory style, that is under conscious control, represents a move toward more flexible thinking. Indeed flexibility of thinking, especially the ability to "reframe" and control or accept thoughts, is an important aspect of personal resilience and the development of positive PWB. When people are troubled by pressures at work there are really only two courses of action that will help them to maintain PWB: change things so that the pressures are alleviated; or change how the pressures are perceived – so that they become less troubling. Which option is practical and desirable will depend on a wide range of different factors. This chapter is focused on how personal development and change can improve resilience and PWB, so here we will concentrate on approaches that change how pressures are perceived. Making actual changes to the work situation is dealt with extensively in other chapters of this book.

Various psychological approaches, originally developed to treat depression, anxiety and related problems have been adapted for use in building resilience and improving PWB at work. The primary approaches that have been used are variations on Cognitive Behaviour Therapies (CBT) and Acceptance and Commitment Training (ACT, Hayes et al., 2006; Luoma et al., 2007). In essence these approaches teach people ways of controlling their thoughts and being able to be more flexible in how they think – and consequently how they feel and act. For example, ACT is designed to enable people to fully experience (rather than avoid or suppress) thoughts, feelings and physiological sensations, especially negatively things such as fear. Rather than wasting precious psychological energy trying to control internal experiences, people accept the feelings and concentrate on achieving their goals. Bond and Bunce (2003) studied a sample of over 400 customer service personnel and showed that acceptance was linked to PWB and an objective measure of performance – over and above the degree of job control that people experienced. The beneficial effects of job control were enhanced when people had higher levels of acceptance. In another study Bond and Bunce (2000) used a true experimental design to assess the impact of ACT training on people working in a media organization. They found improvements in both PWB and a work-related measure of propensity to innovate. CBT approaches also work on cognitive flexibility and the control of thoughts. They focus on helping people to evaluate the accuracy of their beliefs and the relation between their thoughts and feelings. Table 8.2 shows a typical CBT-based tool – a "Thought Record" adapted to enable people to examine the validity of their thinking about work-related issues that trouble them.

One of the most helpful things a thought record can help you to identify is what we call "thinking errors"; a bias toward unhelpful ways of thinking (see Box 8.1 for a bit more information). And before you say anything – we all do them!

Techniques from both ACT and CBT have been adapted and used in developing resilience training for people at work.

Whatever techniques or approaches are used, whether they involve controlling thinking in the kinds of ways described above, or changing the environment by doing something about the external sources of pressure that are troubling someone, it seems clear that individuals who are resilient are very active in finding and using coping strategies. A failure to adopt active coping strategies can lead individuals into a state of "learned helplessness" (see Abramson et al., 1978) where they feel that nothing they can do will alleviate matters and they develop a

TABLE 8.2 **A thought record template**

Situation	Feelings	Thoughts/Beliefs	Challenges and alternatives	Action
What happened or what is happening?	How do you feel about this?	What thoughts are making you feel the way you do? Why do you feel like that?	How rational are your thoughts and beliefs? Are there any Thinking Errors? What's an alternative way to think about this?	What's your best course of action?

set of unhelpful behaviors including withdrawal, resignation and even a resistance to reversing the negative state of affairs.

BOX 8.1 **Thinking errors**

We all have to use short-cuts to draw conclusions and make sense of what is going on around us, based on incomplete information. The following are common thinking errors when they represent a bias toward thinking in a particular way, whatever the objective evidence suggests. Individuals tend to be prone to making one or more of these errors more frequently than the others. It can be very helpful to identify your own bias, and to learn to challenge it by checking out the evidence for and against these thoughts when they occur.

All-or-nothing thinking: You see things in black-and-white categories. For example, if your performance falls short of perfect, you see yourself as a total failure (and similarly for others and their performance). All-or-nothing thinking forms the basis of perfectionism.

Over-generalization: For example, you see a single negative event, such as a career setback, as a never-ending pattern (thinking about it in terms of "always" and "never").

Mental filter: For example, you pick out a single negative detail and dwell on it exclusively, so that your vision of reality becomes darkened.

Jumping to conclusions: You make a (negative) interpretation even though there are no definite facts that convincingly support your conclusion.

Mind reading: You assume you know what other people are thinking, without checking.

Magnification (and minimization): You exaggerate (problems, imperfections etc.)

Emotional reasoning: You take your emotions as evidence for the truth (I feel guilty, therefore I must have done something wrong).

CHALLENGES AND MASTERY EXPERIENCES

As well as using the approaches outlined above to develop more flexible thinking and coping strategies, enhancing resilience is also dependent on taking actions, such as confronting fears and taking on challenges. Research findings support the idea that people's natural levels of resilience are influenced significantly by their early experiences. What the research suggests is that although exposure to serious trauma in early life will not help to build resilience, exposure to experiences that are challenging but mild enough not to inflict lasting damage can actually help to "inoculate" and enhance underlying resilience (e.g. Khoshaba and Maddi, 1999). It seems that exposure to "toughening" experiences may not only promote psychological resilience but also influence underlying neuro-biological mechanisms that underpin psychological resilience (see Haglund et al., 2007).

What this research suggests is that, within reason, experiences that are challenging and create a certain amount of strain are not something to be avoided at all costs. In fact, it seems likely that limited exposure to challenging experiences, especially when the individual feels that he or she has some degree of control, is likely to build, rather than damage resilience. In sport it is commonplace for coaches to push athletes beyond any levels of strain that they may experience in competition to build resilience. One experienced Olympic coach explained this to the authors by saying that, "...if I push them up to and beyond the limit during preparation we then know that there isn't going to be anything that they can't handle in the competition itself". Experiencing challenge and rising to the challenge enables someone to experience "mastery". Experiencing mastery and the sense of achievement that goes along with it is important in building feelings of confidence and competence – both important components in personal resilience. If a challenge is not sufficiently difficult, the feeling of achievement and mastery will not be as deep or as satisfying, but of course (as goal-setting theory established through decades of research – see Chapter 7) the goal needs to be difficult but both attainable and worthwhile. The critical role that a clear "sense of purpose" plays in PWB has been referred to many times, elsewhere in this book. Building and sustaining resilience is also enhanced when there is a clear sense of purpose. If something seems worth striving for it makes coping with adversity to achieve the outcome less troublesome.

When taking on challenging experiences to build resilience, the idea of strengths-based development can be helpful. Strengths-based development focuses on helping people to identify what they are good at and then to develop additional talents, skills and resources around the same areas. Some research has shown that strengths-based development can result in positive behavior change in the workplace (see Hodges and Asplund, 2010 for a review). To build resilience it makes sense to identify experiences that call for the use of existing strengths, rather than taking on something that does not play to a person's strengths, which may turn out to be too challenging and damage, rather than build, resilience.

BACK TO THE BEGINNING – PERSONALITY

As this chapter has illustrated there are many successful approaches that can be taken to develop and build personal resilience. The platform for anyone wishing to develop their resilience is a good understanding of how their underlying personality helps or hinders their personal resilience. As explained elsewhere, psychologists use the FFM as the main structural framework for describing personality but this is not necessarily the most useful framework to use for examining personal resilience. The five factors may be subdivided into a larger number of facets – and it is the mix of these facets (often combining two facets from different "Big Five" factors) that can best show how someone's personality is linked to their resilience. Various key factors, that are based on a combination of "Big Five" facets, such as confidence, social support and adaptability have been shown through existing research to be important in determining personal resilience. Together with colleagues at Robertson Cooper Ltd, the authors have drawn on this research to develop an online expert system for generating a resilience report from a profile of someone's Big Five personality facets. The expert system that generates this report is being constantly updated as new research findings emerge linking personality with resilience. To get your own resilience report, go to www. robertsoncooper.com/iresilience. More information about the current version of the report and the research background to its development can be obtained at www.robertsoncooper.com.

CHAPTER 9

IMPROVING WELL-BEING – BUILDING A HEALTHY WORKPLACE

Earlier chapters in this book have focused on research and evidence. This chapter is more practical and rather than reviewing research findings and introducing new ideas and concepts, it provides guidance on how to take a strategic and practical approach to improving and sustaining PWB in an organization.

The chapters in the next part of the book provide a set of case studies giving real-life illustrations of what has been done in a range of organizations to tackle well-being issues. The case studies vary considerably in scope, in the approaches taken and in the goals that they were designed to achieve. Although not uniform in approach, the case study chapters provide real-life examples of how to use many of the methods, techniques and processes that are part of the generic approach outlined in this chapter and based on material presented throughout this book.

A STRATEGIC APPROACH TO PWB

In any organization there will often be different opportunities and priorities when attempting to enhance PWB. Sometimes it may be sensible to tackle a specific issue, such as high rates of turnover or sickness-absence in a department, rather than to take an organization-wide perspective. In other circumstances, the awareness and capabilities of leadership and management across the whole organization may be the priority, or the recruitment and selection of employees with the resilience to cope with a specific and challenging set of job demands may be an urgent need. Sometimes a strategic approach may be

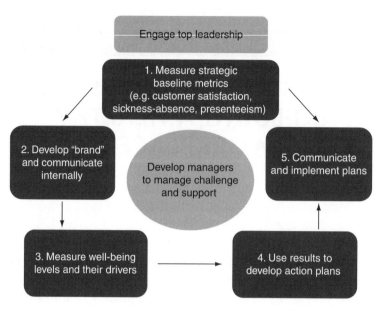

FIGURE 9.1 **A strategic approach to PWB**

extremely desirable but impossible to implement because of a lack of commitment, understanding or recognition from top leadership. The realities of organizational life mean that it is not always feasible, or even desirable, to follow a broad and integrated set of steps toward improved PWB. The approach described in this chapter does give a broad, integrated set of stages, illustrated in Figure 9.1. In some settings, it may be possible and appropriate to follow the whole process from start to finish. For many circumstances it may be best to enter the cycle given in Figure 9.1 at somewhere other than stage one, to omit some of the stages – or even to adopt an entirely different model. Despite these reservations, the model given in this chapter is extremely valuable and provides a useful template for well-being interventions. Its development is based on the experience of working in many different organizations across most sectors of the economy. The case studies in Chapters 10, 11, 14, 15 and 17 all provide good examples of taking a strategic approach in the context of real organizational settings.

In the following sections of this chapter each of the key stages in Figure 9.1 is explained.

ENGAGING TOP LEADERSHIP AND DEVELOPING MANAGERS

The impact of PWB is felt across the whole organization and to be completely successful in harnessing the benefits of high levels of PWB a strategic approach is required. Of necessity all organizations divide up into functional roles and structures. It would be impossible to perform effectively without doing so. The key functional areas that relate to PWB in an organization are Human Resources, Occupational Health, and Health and Safety. For well-being interventions to work really well it is critically important that all three of these functional areas collaborate effectively. This collaboration can only be truly effective if the organization takes a strategic approach to PWB. The benefits of high levels of PWB are potentially substantial but unless an organization takes a strategic approach these benefits may not be fully realized. The reason for this is simple – the benefits of high PWB cross different functional areas. For example, PWB can generate benefits in performance and productivity, sickness-absence rates and talent management. To realize these benefits an HR department needs to include proper consideration of PWB issues in its talent management activities. At the very least this means evaluating recruits, not just from the point of view of skills and abilities, but also ensuring a good match between the demands of the role and the jobholder's resilience profile – and where the match is not good providing support such as resilience training. Health and Safety or Occupational Health may take the lead on dealing with work-related stress but their contribution needs to be linked to management development programs, so that managers are helped to manage effectively for *both* well-being and performance. There are many other examples that could be given to show how the three key functions need to collaborate and not work in silos. The need for this integration explains why, in Figure 9.1, top management commitment and managers' capability to balance challenge and support are not shown as separate stages of the process. They need to be in place throughout the whole set of stages.

A strategic approach to PWB starts with recognition and commitment on the part of the top leadership of the organization. Experience has shown the authors that this is not something that is always easily achieved. Of course no top management team is likely to say that it does not recognize the importance of PWB or that it is not committed to the well-being of its workforce. In practice however, when tackling PWB that requires resources or financial support the espoused commitment may not turn into action. Frequently this is because the top team does not fully grasp the business case for PWB. If you've read all of the previous chapters of this book the business case will be clear – relatively modest investment in PWB can lead to major improvements. The best starting point for any PWB intervention is to ensure that the top leadership team has a proper appreciation of the evidence and the resulting business case. This will make it more likely that the top team will commit resources – and more importantly recognize the importance of a strategic approach, rather than delegating PWB to one of the functional areas. The development of managers to balance challenge and support involves helping them to hold people to account properly but in a way that does not take this to the extreme and become rigid and demoralizing. Similarly they need to be able to recognize when support is needed but not default to this whenever conflict or strain arises – and let people off the hook too easily. As Chapter 7 explains much more fully, effective management and leadership ensures that people are sufficiently challenged, so that they can get the psychologically healthy experience of achieving something difficult – but that support is available to ensure that the challenge does not become impossibly difficult to deal with. The design of a development program for managers can draw on a number of established models and approaches. These include Robertson Cooper's Leadership Impact model, work done on management competencies for preventing and reducing stress at work and work on engaging leadership – all of which are covered in Chapter 7.

MEASURE BASELINE METRICS

A final, essential aspect of a strategic approach to PWB involves identifying the goals of the program and taking baseline measures of these so that the starting point is clear. Being clear about the starting position also enables practical targets and goals for improvement to be set at appropriate levels. Improved PWB has the potential to affect many outcomes for both individual employees and the organization as a whole. For the organization, links have been established between the PWB of employees and a range of important outcomes including: sickness-absence rates; productivity; customer satisfaction and sales performance, but exactly which outcomes are affected will depend on the type of intervention adopted. For example, introducing resilience training for a group of staff which is producing poor results when dealing with particularly challenging service users may help to reduce sickness-absence rates and improve the psychological health and well-being of the staff. It may not have any significant impact on the satisfaction of the service users unless it is coupled with other interventions, such as redesign of working practices, reductions in workload or better goal-setting and monitoring by management.

A good starting point is to prepare a well-being scorecard showing the possible outcomes that could become targets for the intervention. An example of such a scorecard is given in Table 9.1.

Table 9.1 is a scorecard based on the idea of the Balanced Scorecard (Kaplan and Norton, 1996) but focused on outcomes that might be influenced by PWB initiatives. The possible outcomes given in

TABLE 9.1 **A well-being scorecard**

Business level and financial indicators	**Internal process indicators**
■ Sickness Absence rates ■ Retention rates ■ Cost of using agency/contract staff ■ No. of ill-health retirements ■ No. of stress-related referrals to OH ■ Overall financial performance – surplus/break even/deficit ■ Productivity measures	■ Stress levels ■ Levels of work–life balance ■ Stress risk assessment arrangements ■ Staff survey results (job satisfaction, engagement, quality of management and leadership) ■ Take up of health promotion initiatives, e.g. walking clubs, healthy eating ■ Regular high quality appraisals
Quality indicators	**Learning and development indicators**
■ Customer/Patient/User satisfaction survey results ■ Complaints ■ Service quality ratings (internal and external) ■ Product recalls ■ Product performance ■ No. of HSE improvement notices received ■ No. of disciplinaries and grievances	■ Take up and no. of "Did not attends" at training or development events ■ Feedback from leadership development programs ■ Feedback on development – i.e. perceived as effective and relevant ■ Innovations and suggestions ■ Accidents, mistakes and near misses

Table 9.1 are not intended to be comprehensive. They provide an illustration of the type of outcome, in a balanced (i.e. not only financial) set of four categories. The key point here is that the first step, even before a PWB initiative begins, is to identify very clearly WHY it is being undertaken and, in particular, which outcomes are expected to change as a consequence. This seems an obvious point to make but in our experience it is quite common for organizations to begin in a piecemeal way, without being clear about what results are expected. Another important issue is to be realistic about how much impact can realistically be expected. For example, conducting a stress survey, with follow-up in areas where high levels of absence are reported, will probably have a beneficial impact but it is unlikely to drastically reduce sickness-absence across the board, or have a major impact on customer satisfaction. So, on the one hand, it's important to consider all of the possible areas where improved PWB could bring benefits but it is also important to be realistic about this, in the light of the specific PWB program that is planned.

BRANDING AND COMMUNICATION

A coherent and recognizable brand for a PWB program is an important ingredient for overall success. It is not unusual for an organization to be undertaking well-being initiatives that are not recognized as such. Examples include the provision of a telephone counseling service (employee assistance program), recognition and awards ceremonies, subsidized gym membership and stress management training. It is also common for various disparate well-being interventions to be undertaken by different functional areas across the organization – without any clear strategic connection. This takes us back to the point about the need for a strategic approach to well-being. One benefit of taking a strategic approach focused on a set of clear goals and outcome objectives is that it enables any existing initiatives to be recognized and drawn together within the new interventions to provide a coherent program, within an overall well-being brand. As explained in Chapter 3, for employees to be fully engaged with their organization they need to feel that the organization cares about their well-being. Recognition of what the organization is actually doing is much easier and more likely to be visible to employees if there is an overall positive brand that pulls together the well-being initiatives, under a catchy label such as "LFB Healthy" (Chapter 15, see also Chapters 12 and 14). In practice, since the brand needs to reflect and incorporate the program of PWB activities, it is often better to finalize the brand and the full set of initiatives after the next stage of the process – measurement. Ideally, a full (evidence-based) understanding of current levels of PWB in an organization precedes the development of an intervention program. In practice of course, as already noted, this is not always how things are done.

MEASURE WELL-BEING LEVELS AND THEIR DRIVERS

Chapter 5 provides a detailed account of the measurement of PWB in the workplace. As Chapter 5 explains, the best way to obtain a clear picture of current levels of PWB and information about the key organization drivers of PWB is to conduct a well-being audit. Chapters 10 and 15 provide case study examples of the use of a well-being audit.

The measurement of PWB using an organization-wide audit tool such as ASSET (see Chapter 5) is not an end in itself, although the UK government Foresight Mental Capital and Wellbeing Project (2008) produced evidence to show that even when an audit was conducted with no follow-up, benefits of almost £2 for every £1 spent were realized. The real purpose in measuring PWB levels and the organizational enablers and barriers is to provide a basis for action. The information obtained through the audit must be seen in the context of the goals set for the PWB interventions and the plans and strategy for the organization. For example, plans for the acquisition of a new division, the recent closure of a unit or a goal to improve productivity levels will all have implications for how the well-being results are seen and will influence the development of an action plan based on the results. As noted in Chapter 5, it also usually makes sense to supplement the questionnaire data with information from focus group discussions. Focus groups can be particularly useful if they take place after the audit, so that points emerging from them can be explored in more depth – and suggestions for action can be elicited from participants.

USE RESULTS TO DEVELOP ACTION PLANS

According to evidence collected during the Foresight project (Foresight, 2008), when a well-being audit is conducted and there is follow-up action the benefits are significant. Once the results are available and have been interpreted in the context of organizational strategy and the goals of PWB interventions, an action plan can be developed. A critical consideration, when it comes to implementing PWB initiatives, is to ensure that any changes made are seen as fair and equitable across the whole organization. Whether something is fair or not is best examined from two key perspectives – referred to as distributive justice and procedural justice (see Colquitt et al., 2005). An organizational change that is seen to unfairly reward, or disadvantage, someone is breaking the rules of distributive justice – the actual distribution of rewards is unfair. Of course, sometimes in an organization it is appropriate to treat an individual or group differently. In this case, it is critical that the process (procedural justice) for deciding who should receive the reward is seen to be fair.

There is no simple prescription for what action should be taken. What is needed depends on the organization in question, its goals, history and the specific results obtained. Although there is no simple prescription, it is possible to identify broad types of interventions that might be considered. One useful way of categorizing interventions is to consider primary, secondary and tertiary interventions.

As Figure 9.2 shows the most difficult and resource-intensive interventions are primary-level interventions. These are challenging for organizations because they involve a level of change that is more

---

PWB interventions: Levels of Intervention

Primary Level

- Aimed at enhancing the work situation to improve the impact on individuals, e.g. job redesign, culture change, flexible working, work–life balance policies

Secondary Level

- Increasing the awareness, resilience and coping skills of the individuals and making some changes to the situation, e.g. through better leadership and management. Interventions might include better recruitment and selection process, management development focused on managing for well-being, stress management training and positive health promotion activities

Tertiary Level

- Support or treatment for individuals experiencing problems with PWB – without making changes to the work situation e.g. counselling, return to work policies

---

FIGURE 9.2 **PWB interventions: Levels of intervention**

fundamental and may call for changes to how people's jobs are done, changes to working processes and practices that are well-established. Proposals for primary-level interventions are also more likely to lead to resistance from within the organization, since they may require individuals and groups of employees to take on different roles, ways of working or responsibilities. This definitely does not imply that primary-level interventions are less valuable. In fact if taken seriously and implemented with the full commitment of top leadership they have the potential to produce the biggest pay-off. In practice, organizations generally find it less challenging to introduce secondary- and tertiary-level interventions. In organizations where PWB is a problem tertiary interventions may already be in place to help support already distressed individuals. Secondary-level interventions often enable organizations to tackle PWB issues and make substantial improvements, without the challenge and upheaval of primary interventions – but with more lasting preventative impact than tertiary interventions. There are many examples of very effective secondary-level interventions in the case studies in the later part of this book. Chapter 17, for example, uses a slightly different framework to categorize interventions but provides a very clear example of an organization-wide strategic approach using a range of different interventions. Chapter 18 gives a case study focused on using innovative leadership development to keep pressure positive.

COMMUNICATE AND IMPLEMENT PLANS

The importance of pulling together well-being initiatives into a coherent overall brand and communicating effectively across the organization has already been explained. The communication process is particularly important when interventions are being introduced. One critical point here concerns how the purpose of the interventions is communicated within the organization. Chapter 3 examines the relationships between employee engagement and PWB. It also explains the trap that senior leadership can fall into, of focusing on a narrow "business benefits" view of engagement and well-being. Of course high levels of PWB bring benefits for the organization. That has been one of the core messages of this book. But there are also important benefits for everyone who works in an organization – and these are the priority messages that need to accompany any intervention. Top leadership needs to recognize that improving PWB for each person in the organization will deliver positive results for the organization – but there may be a lag between interventions and results. The top team also needs to resist the natural temptation to focus only on the "business benefit" angle. Ideally, communications about the PWB interventions and the resulting benefits need to genuinely prioritize the benefits to the people in the organization – whilst also honestly recognizing that this will deliver organizational benefits. In this way PWB interventions can be elevated beyond something designed to improve employee engagement or commitment or any of the "business benefits" led interventions – all of which run the risk of being seen as a management ploy to get more out of people – to become an endeavor that is "win-win" and provides something that can be wholeheartedly pursued for the mutual benefit of the organization and its members.

PART 5

CASE STUDIES

The case studies that follow provide a varied and broad set of examples. We are extremely grateful to the authors of these case studies and to the host organizations for giving permission for the reports to be published. The chapters that follow give real-world illustrations of many of the points that are discussed at a more conceptual level in the earlier chapters of this book. Each case study is complete in its own right and is designed to give a self-contained, real-life account of interventions that are designed to improve PWB. In some cases the interventions have quite a wide focus and cover PWB in the context of overall health and well-being (i.e. including physical health). Other cases are more tightly focused on PWB as such. As already noted in the previous chapter the case studies do not all follow the sequence described in Figure 9.1 but many of the different stages given in Figure 9.1 are reflected in the different chapters that follow.

A brief description of what each case covers is given below. The description given is simply intended to provide a succinct orientation for the reader and certainly does not reflect the full scope of any of the cases in the chapters that follow. Reading them is the only way to get the full benefit of the extensive material in the case studies!

Chapter 10 describes an intervention program that includes the use of a full-scale well-being audit and follow-up management development activity.

Chapters 11, 13 and 14 look at the implementation of broad well-being programs in specific organizations. Chapter 11 focuses on a multinational organization, Chapter 13 on a chemical company in Germany and Chapter 14 on a university in England.

Chapters 12 and 16 do not describe an intervention in a specific organization, they offer general guidance on the introduction of health and well-being initiatives. Chapter 16 looks specifically at online interventions.

Chapter 17 describes the introduction of a comprehensive well-being program developed following the results of a well-being audit.

Chapter 18 describes the introduction of a well-being theme into a leadership development program.

Chapter 10 – Improving Employee Engagement and Well-Being in an NHS Trust
Gordon Tinline and Nick Hayter, Robertson Cooper Ltd, and *Kim Crowe*, Mersey Care NHS Trust

Chapter 11 – Building an Organizational Culture of Health
Scott Ratzen, Johnson & Johnson USA

Chapter 12 – Engaging in Health and Well-Being
Jessica Colling, Vielife

Chapter 13 – The Development of a Comprehensive Corporate Health Management System for Well-Being
Karl Kuhn and Klaus Pelster, Germany

Chapter 14 – The Journey Toward Organizational Resilience at the University of Leeds
Nina Quinlan and Gary Tideswell, Higher Education HEFCE Consortium Project, University of Leeds

Chapter 15 – Improving Well-Being at London Fire Brigade
Mairin Finn, London Fire Brigade and *Gordon Tinline*, Robertson Cooper Ltd

Chapter 16 – On the Use of Internet-Delivered Interventions in Worksite Health Promotion
Rik Crutzen, CAPHRI, Maastricht University, The Netherlands

Chapter 17 – Mitigating the Impact of an Economic Downturn on Mental Well-Being
Paul Litchfield, BT Group plc

Chapter 18 – Keeping Pressure Positive: Improving Well-Being and Performance in the NHS Through Innovative Leadership Development
Jill Flint-Taylor, Robertson Cooper Ltd, Joan Durose, Health Services Management Center, University of Birmingham and Caroline Wigley, NHS West Midlands

CHAPTER 10

IMPROVING EMPLOYEE ENGAGEMENT AND WELL-BEING IN AN NHS TRUST

Gordon Tinline and Nick Hayter
Robertson Cooper Ltd

and

Kim Crowe
Mersey Care NHS Trust

OVERVIEW

Mersey Care NHS Trust partnered with Robertson Cooper to design and implement an integrated leadership development and employee well-being program. This was introduced at a time during which the Trust was going through a major change and restructuring process, having recently begun their application to attain status as Foundation Trust equivalent. A priority of the program was to ensure that employees felt involved and supported throughout the restructure and felt good about coming to work. In light of this Robertson Cooper designed a program to measure the levels of Psychological Well-Being (PWB), engagement and perceived productivity of employees, using the ASSET framework (see Chapter 5). The leadership development process was then designed to incorporate ASSET results so that action plans could be made to improve well-being and engagement in the priority areas, as well as informing managers about how to become more effective leaders. Of the senior managers and clinicians who completed the evaluation, 83 percent agreed that the content of the development centers met their expectations. Subsequent monitoring of performance of the Clinical Business Units has seen an improvement in key performance indicators and some measures have significantly exceeded original targets. There are now plans to re-use ASSET to assess the impact of the change, which will lead to further evaluation and progress toward the full objectives of the program.

BACKGROUND

Mersey Care NHS Trust provides specialist mental health and learning disability services for the people of Liverpool, Sefton and Kirkby. Mersey Care is one of the three UK mental health trusts with a high secure unit. The Trust was facing a number of significant strategic challenges including the pursuit of Foundation Trust equivalent (FTe) status and organizational restructuring into new Clinical Business Units (CBUs). This led Mersey Care's Chief Executive to commission Robertson Cooper to help ensure that staff were as prepared as possible to meet these strategic challenges in terms of well-being and engagement, and that management achieved effective leadership goals.

Within the context of the NHS, the emphasis on employee health and well-being has recently been reinforced by the Boorman review.[1] This review emphasizes the need for NHS organizations to take a strategic, co-ordinated and pro-active approach toward looking after the health and well-being of their employees, if they are to successfully support the health of the nation. The Final Boorman report summarizes the key areas that are prerequisites for employee health and well-being – the most relevant of which for this case study are the following areas:

- Embedding a fuller definition of employee health, well-being and engagement in the core business of the organization;
- The need for broad commitment toward health, well-being and engagement by, for example, providing core health and well-being services as well as additional services targeted at the needs of the organization;
- Proper resourcing of employee health and well-being services by, for example, ensuring senior management ownership, developing and equipping managers and involving employees at all levels.

THE APPROACH

Aims and objectives

The Trust was aiming to achieve FTe status, which is a new standard of excellence for NHS organizations. If successful, the Trust will remain under the control of central government, but work in a similar way to Foundation Trusts and be empowered to deliver high-quality services to local people who have greater influence over their health service provision.

In attempting to achieve FTe status, the Trust also aims to demonstrate good governance and financial sustainability. To achieve sustainable change during the restructure, the Trust also installed a tough new financial plan and targets for delivering greater efficiencies and increased productivity. The Trust recognized that restructuring and imposing new targets would have an impact on employees at all levels. A priority was to ensure that employees felt involved and supported throughout the restructure as well as feeling good about coming to work and being engaged in their roles. Also, a leadership development process was designed with the aim of equipping leaders to better understand the impact they have, and recognize the changes they may need to make, to enhance the well-being and engagement of their employees.

The program

Measuring employee well-being

The starting point was to carry out a well-being survey of all employees, using ASSET, to provide a comprehensive and detailed profile of the barriers and enablers of well-being across the Trust with differences highlighted by department, location, length of service and other demographic groups.

The survey was not only used as a baseline measure. The ASSET reports also helped leaders identify priorities and build action plans to improve well-being and engagement. The results made available to leaders enable them to see how *their* employees feel in critical areas such as relationships at work, workload and sense of purpose. Importantly, these are areas that the leaders could influence for themselves provided that they develop the right skills (and are provided with adequate resources).

Leadership development centers

ASSET data were used to feed into the leadership development process so that leaders were challenged to think about the impact they had, and where relevant, the changes they needed to make to enhance the well-being of their employees.

To remain context specific, the leadership development program was also based on the NHS Leadership Qualities Framework (LQF), but this was reduced to four core dimensions. The LQF is an established leadership competency framework widely used in the NHS. However, like many such competency frameworks, it has too many dimensions (N = 16) to be applied effectively in a limited development context. Therefore, a content analysis of the framework was applied to cluster the competencies into four core areas:

- Self-Development (internal focus);
- Drive and Motivation (external focus);
- Leading through People;
- Strategic Capacity.

This reduced model was easier to apply in a one-day Development Center and was well-received not just by Mersey Care but also by HR professionals from other Trusts who acted as observers at the events.

The leadership development process used Development Centres (DCs) which are well-established adaptations of Assessment Center (AC) methods, with participants working through a number of observed structured exercises (for example, group discussions, role plays, in-tray exercises). However, DCs are usually very focused on the individuals' development needs in relative isolation from the organizational context. In this program, we were keen to encompass the latter by including a focus on developing leadership that was directly targeted at improving employee well-being and engagement. By including reflection and peer mentoring we allowed participants to carefully consider the relevance of the DC experience to their career progression at a time of substantial organizational change and restructuring. To enable these objectives to be realized a second Robertson

Cooper assessment tool, Leadership Impact (LI), was used as part of the DC process.

The LI tool is a personality assessment based on the "Big Five" model of personality, which is the most widely recognized and used personality model. In the model there are five stable elements to personality and people have different natural preferences for each. The five elements are openness, conscientiousness, extraversion, agreeableness and neuroticism (see Chapters 4 and 6 for more information on personality and the Big Five model). LI does not report explicitly on these areas, but uses the leaders' scores to provide feedback on their impact on the engagement and well-being of their workgroups.

All senior managers and clinicians attending the DCs completed the questionnaire. The LI report provides feedback to managers on their natural leadership style and how it impacts the key areas that determine employee well-being and engagement (the same areas measured by ASSET). The participants were encouraged to consider their Leadership Impact profiles in relation to the well-being and engagement levels of the actual workgroups that they led – as revealed by the relevant ASSET survey results. This process, developed by Robertson Cooper, is known as Vector Analysis (see Box 10.1 for more information). The DCs were one-day events held off-site in the period October 2008–February 2009 and were open to all senior managers and clinicians likely to play a leadership role in the new CBUs.

BOX 10.1 **Vector analysis: Connecting leadership directly to staff engagement and well-being**

Vector Analysis is a process that brings together an assessment of the natural leadership style of a manager with an assessment of the well-being and engagement levels of the staff he or she leads. It provides a simultaneous focus on leadership development and staff well-being and engagement. Two assessment tools are used as the basis for the Vector Analysis process, *Leadership Impact* and *ASSET*.

- *Leadership Impact* is a personality-based assessment of the leader, which shows his/her likely impact on the workgroup. Leadership Impact reports on the leader's natural style in terms of the balance she/he is likely to strike between challenging people and supporting them. It focuses on leadership

---

BOX 10.1 **(Continued)**

strengths and highlights the risks of overusing strengths without flexing his/her approach. The report is structured around six key areas that a leader must impact positively to ensure that his/her people feel motivated, energized, resilient and above all, able to deliver high performance.

■ *ASSET* is a short questionnaire completed by the leader's workgroup (for example direct reports). It measures the workgroup's perception of the workplace in terms of what is blocking or enabling productivity and performance. It provides a real "view from the floor" based on an established model of the factors that impact performance at work.

The Vector Analysis process brings together the results from *Leadership Impact* with those from *ASSET*. It provides a common framework to report on the leader's likely impact and the key situational factors that drive performance and well-being. Vector Analysis provides insight for leaders that opens up a process of personal development that can deliver benefits for the leader and the workgroup alike. The combined results from the two assessments provide a powerful process for developing leaders and workgroups to bring about measurable performance improvements in both, with a strong focus on the areas that are critical to well-being and engagement (for example, collaborative relationships, well-managed change, balanced workload and so on).

OUTCOMES AND EVALUATION

Generally, the DC approach was well-received, for example 75 percent of participants agreed that they found the DCs useful for their personal development and 83 percent agreed that the content of the DCs met their expectations. This data were gathered through a post-DC evaluation survey.

In order to meet the broader aims and objectives of the program, the Trust has put in place routine "governance checks" in which the CBUs report their progress toward key performance indicators. These include financial and productivity targets as well as other measures such as reducing absence rates and ensuring employee engagement and well-being are high. The overall CBU performance to date has been very encouraging and the latest measures show an improvement in all areas.

Overall, CBU performance in certain key performance indicators, including financial viability, has already exceeded original targets.

However, there was one CBU that was not performing to agreed targets. The CBU in question was left to its own devices, whilst being made aware that support was available if needed. Additional support to enable the CBU to improve performance was given with the senior leaders still taking responsibility for improvement. In taking this "enlightened" approach, the senior management team had demonstrated to the CBU that the leaders and employees are critical in the running of their business area for themselves, whereas before, the approach of the senior management team may have been to intervene at an earlier stage. In this example, the CBU has since made significant improvements, but continues to have additional monitoring from the senior management team.

There are still challenges ahead to build on the initial success of the program and the positive reactions that it has inspired. There are a number of planned activities to embed the actions and more fully evaluate the program, including the following:

- Achieving FTe status: the Trust continues to participate in the Development Phase of the application process and has finalized a Membership Strategy, Constitution document and Election; is making arrangements to hold their first Members Council elections; is finalizing the content of the Trust's 5-year Integrated Business Plan (IBP); and is preparing for the final stages of the application process. Achieving FTe status is an important outcome in the successfulness of the program.
- Improving leadership performance: by revisiting the *Leadership Impact* data at a CBU senior leadership team level. Facilitated workshops will be offered to continue the support and development offered to leadership teams. The focus will be on considering the collective leadership impact that the senior leadership teams have on the engagement and well-being of their business units. Leaders will also be asked to feedback their views about the successfulness of the DCs in increasing their learning, changing their behavior and improving their performance as a leader, as well as suggesting areas where they feel further support is required. This is an important component in the continued development of the leadership teams.
- Re-configuring the ASSET data: so that the reporting tool can provide summaries for the new CBU's. This will provide insight into the potential key barriers to and enablers of well-being and engagement for each CBU (based on staff responses collected prior to the

restructure). These results will aid the implementation of evidence-based action planning with the right interventions targeted in the right areas. This data will also provide a valid baseline measurement that can be used as a comparison point for evaluating progress over time.

- Repeating the full employee ASSET survey: the results from this survey will provide a key evaluation metric in establishing how far Mersey Care has come in improving staff engagement and well-being. One challenge will be improving on the 33 percent response rate in the last ASSET survey, as this in itself can be a strong indicator of staff engagement. (The target for the next ASSET survey is for half of all staff to submit responses, which is in-line with the 49 percent response rate achieved in the most recent NHS Staff Survey.) It is hoped that the active use of the results of the last ASSET survey, particularly through leadership development, will encourage more staff to respond on the basis that they consider the survey to be a meaningful and useful staff consultation exercise.
- The Trust has appointed a Staff Health and Well-being manager to coordinate this area of work and has appointed the Director of Workforce as a Staff Health and Well-being Champion at Trust Board level.

SUMMARY

The Trust started the program before the Boorman review, but the process that was used dovetails very well with the final recommendations, in that the program helps to achieve the following:

- *Embedding a fuller definition of employee health, well-being and engagement in the core business of the organization*: The Trust continues to use the ASSET framework, which measures the broader aspects of employee health, well-being and engagement.
- *The need for broad commitment toward health, well-being and engagement*: In carrying out ASSET and the leadership development program, the Trust is better able to identify the priority areas for action as well as which "levers" to pull in order to embed and improve the intended outcomes.
- *Proper resourcing of employee health and well-being services*: The program has demonstrated senior management ownership in the health

and well-being of employees, as well as commitment to develop and equip leaders. In opting to repeat ASSET, all employees will be invited to share their views on the impact of the program, and also help to identify priority areas for further improvement.

The integrated program has given Mersey Care a strong basis for ensuring that leadership development is focused on employee engagement and well-being. However, there is still substantial work to undertake to ensure this becomes the norm within the Trust and there are a number of barriers to overcome to achieve this goal. One of these barriers is the wide range of leadership development approaches and models the NHS is exposed to, and to some degree, generates. The factors that underpin employee engagement and well-being, such as strong relationships, ensuring a sense of purpose and managing workloads and change effectively tend to be constants in complex organizations. Mersey Care, like other NHS Trusts, has to rise to the challenge of ensuring that it keeps these factors firmly at the heart of leadership development and practice, while being able to take account of new thinking that emerges over the coming years.

CHAPTER 11

BUILDING AN ORGANIZATIONAL CULTURE OF HEALTH

Fikry Isaac
Executive Director, Global Health Services and Chief Medical Officer,
Johnson & Johnson, USA

and

Scott Ratzen
Vice President Global Health, Johnson & Johnson, USA

OVERVIEW

Given that Johnson & Johnson is the largest health care company in the world, it stands to reason that it would extend the same level of excellence it is known to have for its health and wellness products, to the health and wellness of its own employees. By adopting the philosophies of "caring for the world one person at a time", the Johnson & Johnson health and wellness programs reach around the globe, and touch employees' homes. The programs aim at prevention, but are also constructed to respond without judgment, and treat the individual throughout the health continuum. It has strived for – and achieved – a "culture of health" throughout the corporation that is spreading into the communities in which employees live and work. This case study focuses on the components of Johnson & Johnson's "Health and Wellness Program".

BACKGROUND

The organization

Johnson & Johnson is a decentralized corporation broken into three business segments: Medical Devices and Diagnostics (the world's largest medical technology business), Pharmaceuticals (seventh largest pharmaceutical business and fourth largest biotech) and Consumer (considered the "premier" consumer health care business) (see Johnson & Johnson, 2009). Johnson & Johnson has over 119,000 employees working in 57 countries. Their products are marketed in over 175 nations. The company delivered a shareholder return of over 11 percent in 2009, continuing to outperform most stock indices.

The philosophy

The Credo, developed by General Robert Wood Johnson over 60 years ago, drives decisions throughout the corporation, at every level, and in all companies and departments. Most relevant to health and wellness are these clauses:

We are responsible to our employees, the men and women who work with us throughout the world. Everyone must be considered as an individual. We must respect their dignity and recognize their merit...We must be mindful of ways to help our employees fulfil their family responsibilities...We must encourage civic improvements and better health and education.

With the Credo in mind, Johnson & Johnson set out a few decades ago to create a "culture of health", in which employees make healthy choices on the job and in their home lives. The company saw this as the only way to achieve long-term corporate health; wellness initiatives needed to be seen as the means to positive lifestyle changes rather than short-term programs. A premise behind Johnson & Johnson's wellness initiatives is that *the health of the individual is inseparable from the health of the corporation*. Achieving a culture of health leaves a wellness and prevention legacy to future generations of corporate employees and their families.

THE APPROACH

Those who think the notion of creating a healthy workplace is a fairly recent phenomenon have not read the story of Johnson & Johnson's Company Group Chairman, Jim Burke. He was the impetus behind piloting LIVE FOR LIFE® in 1978. Burke believed that unhealthy behaviors such as smoking, overeating, alcohol abuse, emotional stress, hypertension and unsafe driving were responsible for a large share of the company's health care costs in the United States. Over 50 percent of employees voluntarily participated in the pilot program (Isaac, 2001). Wellness programs have been available to Johnson & Johnson employees ever since, with the results being measured since 1995, when LIVE FOR LIFE® was recast as the Health & Wellness Program. Today, these initiatives are global and recognized as Global Health Services. The Global Health Services group is made up of several doctors and nurses, professionals in employee assistance and occupational health, health promotion personnel and medical managers. Onsite occupational health clinics, which focus exclusively on ensuring the safety and health of working people, are a focal point for delivery of health programs and services.

Currently the Johnson & Johnson Sustainability report, and its website, list eight detailed descriptions of health-related interventions provided to employees: Mental Well-Being (employee assistance program, EAP), *Healthy People* (health improvement), Healthy Working Environment (occupational health), HIV/AIDS Initiatives, Workplace Safety, Ergonomics, Fleet Safety and CEO Cancer Gold Standard (cancer prevention). However, that list does not fully reflect the dozens of other programs and processes that are in place to encourage and sustain healthy employees, such as:

- Online Health Profile (annual health risk assessment)
- Lifestyle/disease management counseling
- Health Risk Intervention programs
- Environmental/cultural support
- Financial Incentives for participation
- Integration of health promotion strategy with health care benefit plan design
- On-site fitness centers, and fitness and lifestyle coaching
- Nutritional options in company cafeterias.

The goal of the Global Health initiative is: "Have the healthiest, most engaged workforce – allowing for full and productive lives". That translates to reducing health risk factors, medical and pharmaceutical costs, and hospital admissions, as well as increasing doctor office calls and prescription drug use, which are signs of appropriate care.

An important ongoing initiative, which emerged out of the Health & Wellness Program in 2000, is referred to as "Healthy People". In 2009, it had an 83 percent participation rate in the US. *Healthy People* is a massive undertaking that is managed and implemented by a team of health and wellness professionals, along with outside consultants and suppliers that provide everything from individual health risk assessments and disease management to nutritional planning for on-site company cafeterias.

More specifically, *Healthy People* has set goals in four target areas:

- Reduce smoking/tobacco use
- Reduce high blood pressure (below 140/90)
- Reduce high cholesterol (below 240 total)
- Increase physical activity (at least 30 minutes, 3 times/week).

It is in these four areas that *Healthy People* has made an impact, as these most directly affect the top health risk areas not just at Johnson & Johnson, but across the global population.

Real stories, real people

Another important way to keep employees engaged and at peak performance is by partnering with Wellness & Prevention, Inc., a company owned by Johnson & Johnson. Wellness & Prevention, Inc. is focused on delivering an integrated and comprehensive set of health and performance products and services to companies in order to connect employees with the resources they need to improve their lifestyle. Johnson & Johnson employees can reap the benefits of this partnership by accessing a number of their offerings which allow for a tailored, individualized approach to wellness.

The goals of Wellness & Prevention are to: prevent onset of chronic disease, sustain health and well-being and restore faculties lost to aging. Its purpose is perfectly aligned with everything the

Global Health Services group is trying to do with *Healthy People*. Synchronously they are driving healthy lifestyles for employees, their families and retired personnel as well (see Boxes 11.1 and 11.2).

BOX 11.1 A success story

One employee used Wellness & Prevention's support to make life-changing positive changes. An attorney at Johnson & Johnson, she struggled with her weight most of her life. When the company asked if employees wanted to participate in a corporate wellness plan to make sustainable changes, she jumped at the chance. She began her program with a visit to the Human Performance Institute, a company acquired by Wellness & Prevention in 2008. There she learned about incorporating exercise into her life. Afterward, the Wellness & Prevention team provided access to a gym, a personal trainer and an improvement plan. In less than a year she lost eight inches around her waist and cut her visceral body fat in half. She says in a video posted on the Johnson & Johnson YouTube health channel:

> J&J really does support the health of its employees. J&J puts it money where its mouth is...I am empowered to make whatever changes I want in my health and my future. I am in control. It's a pretty amazing feeling.

BOX 11.2 Another success story

Another success story is about a retired Johnson & Johnson employee who worked as an occupational health nurse manager. She continued to use the company's site fitness centers, which are available to retirees as part of its Credo commitment to ensuring an ongoing healthy lifestyle. She found a trainer whose "gentle enthusiasm" encouraged her to make exercise a regular habit. After a recent serious fall where she sustained a broken leg, she was told that her pre-injury conditioning enabled shorter rehabilitation, and she returned to her usual active lifestyle compared with others her age.

Beyond the data, these are the stories that tell us *Healthy People* is working, and well worth our investment. Today, we see employee health and well-being becoming a part of business strategy for the sustainability of Johnson & Johnson. It is now accepted at all levels across the organization that *the health of the individual is inseparable from the health of the corporation.*

Public awareness of excellence

Johnson & Johnson has achieved various awards over the years for implementing health and wellness programs, all of which reflect the achievement of a culture of health. The CEO Roundtable on Cancer Prevention chaired by our CEO William Weldon, in 2006, honored Johnson & Johnson as one of the first companies to earn the *CEO Cancer Gold Standard*™ accreditation in recognition of building a culture of health and wellness. In the same year, the National Business Group on Health recognized Johnson & Johnson with the platinum award for the company's commitment to help create a healthy workforce through meaningful fitness and lifestyle improvement programs.

To confirm the efficacy of these programs, a team of external researchers recently offered additional validation of Johnson & Johnson's success, revealing: reduced prevalence of high-risk factors (such as obesity, hypertension and tobacco use); significantly lower average growth in medical and pharmaceutical costs; health risk trends better than national norms; and a confirmed return on investment for every dollar spent toward program initiatives.

OUTCOMES AND EVALUATION

Anyone reading this book is already aware of the value of corporate health and wellness programs. Johnson & Johnson's is no exception. It has produced healthier and happier employees around the world, and has avoided costs in the millions of dollars. However, there are some aspects of Johnson & Johnson's initiative that make it stand out amongst its peer programs. There are four in particular:

1. It is a *global* initiative, not just in the United States.
2. It extends its reach to employees' *families*.
3. It has made employees of Johnson & Johnson *healthier* than the population.
4. It *avoids medical and other costs.*

It's global

Managing a health and wellness program outside the United States is a formidable challenge. Nonetheless, Johnson & Johnson's programs are known and working in every country in which there is a company facility. Employees around the globe, at every level, are health literate, and recognize that they are responsible for their own health. This has occurred despite:

- regional barriers (language, cultural norms)
- regional regulations (privacy/confidentiality, local policies)
- local operations (presence or lack of stakeholder support, management engagement, budgets, staffing)
- technology (varying levels of systems and savvy)
- different health risk priorities.

Some challenges and their solutions are noteworthy. For instance, Japan, with a large population of smokers, had difficulty achieving the corporate-instituted tobacco-free policy by 2007. So efforts were made to help the workforce understand the measures required to create a smoke-free place, beginning with separating smoking areas. Additional tools were provided to support tobacco management using company Intranet, symposiums, promotion and a comprehensive smoking cessation program (counseling, workshops and nicotine replacement). Johnson & Johnson's Asian facilities are now 100 percent tobacco-free.

One of the greatest challenges to Johnson & Johnson in expanding their health culture around the globe was the Employee Assistance Program (EAP). Johnson & Johnson's EAP consists of individual counseling, preventative screenings, resilience training, critical incident interventions and management consultations to help mitigate the human and organizational suffering that results from business, personal and environmental challenges. EAP is a new concept in many countries outside of the United States.

A good EAP that addresses overwhelming life issues can yield measurable results including financial savings, decreased employee absence and improved productivity at work. Providing EAP services worldwide required overcoming a number of hurdles including:

- Lack of familiarity with the concept of EAP, requiring extensive education
- Removing the stigma related to mental health or personal issues

- Managing over 25 vendors across countries and cultures, and assuring quality
- Taking into account cultural sensitivities in program delivery
- Customizing to account for cultural diversity.

As of 2009, Johnson & Johnson has made EAP accessible to 100 percent of its employees across North America and Australia, 98 percent in Asia, 88 percent in Latin America and 81 percent in Europe, Africa and the Middle East.

It includes employees' families

Many of Johnson & Johnson's employee programs are extended to its family members. In addition to aligning with the Credo commitment to help "employees fulfil their family responsibilities", it makes sense to turn healthy living into a household-wide activity. Enabling employees to use family members as partners in their efforts to improve health, maximizes the likelihood of success. Furthermore, a healthy family reduces family insurance claims.

The programs available to spouses include smoking cessation, an online service that offers confidential health profiles and coaching sessions and training in defensive driving. A company website allows employees and spouses to log and monitor their exercise routines, calculate calorie counts and read articles related to their health interests. A popular part of Johnson & Johnson's outreach to families of their employees is an arrangement with a nation-wide network of fitness centers. Partners and dependents can be eligible for club membership, weight-loss programs and home-fitness options.

One of the ways Johnson & Johnson creatively motivates families to participate in *Healthy People* is by offering financial incentives (e.g., discounts on medical plan contributions) when selected preventative programs have been completed.

Besides providing the support of a loved one while making healthy choices at home, spousal involvement impacts the bottom line. Employee spouses and dependents incur over 25 percent of health care claim costs, and account for around half of the cost of health care coverage for an employer. This justifies the additional expense of providing services to the entire family.

Employees are healthier than most

It's a strong statement to make, but Johnson & Johnson employees are considerably healthier than the US population. The company's data compare favorably with other companies who have health and wellness programs, too. Some notable statistics for Johnson & Johnson employees:

- The rate of heart disease is 41 percent below national standards.
- High blood pressure is 75 percent below national standards (Health and Wellness at Johnson & Johnson, youtube.com).
- They are more active than the national average.
- They smoke less (Rowh, 2010).

In 2000, Johnson & Johnson took on the challenge of setting goals to align with the U.S. Department of Health and Human Services' *Healthy People 2010*. Both focused on the same four health indicators. Johnson & Johnson's employee population had fewer health risks when they started measuring, but they also improved much more with the use of the company's health initiatives over the same period of time as the general population (see Table 11.1).

Looking specifically at the four areas targeted by the *Healthy People* initiative, and studied by the company as well as outside researchers, these positive findings show the success of the health initiatives over time.

Achieving results takes time, but can yield early wins. Sustaining them requires consistency in programming, regular monitoring of satisfaction and ongoing improvement goals. Companies who invest in wellness programs need to be prepared to wait for a measurable return on their investment.

TABLE 11.1   **Health risk indicator improvement at Johnson & Johnson over time**

	1995–1999	2002	2007	2009
Tobacco use	12%	8.5%	4.0%	3.9%
High blood pressure	14%	12.2%	6.6%	6.3%
High cholesterol	19%	10.4%	7.0%	5.3%
Inactivity	39%	40.5%	33.5%	20.4%

Prevention adds up to more than dollars and cents. Employees tell us all the time what a huge difference our programs have made for them – how they've beaten back obesity, gained control over high blood pressure, started breathing better, and taken up exercise. There's no value you can put on this.

– William C. Weldon, CEO, Johnson & Johnson, April 12, 2010

Avoids costs associated with illness

While many companies are only beginning to recognize the value of health and wellness programs, Johnson & Johnson has encouraged health for decades. Since the company began accurately measuring health care costs in the context of a health program, it estimates having avoided millions in health care costs based on about $225 saved per employee per year for reduced health care utilization (Ozminkowski, 2002).

Over the years of seeing health improvements and watching insurance premiums, we believe that 70 percent of health care costs could be prevented through lifestyle modification (Arnst, 2009).

The bottom-line health care savings is only one positive output of Johnson & Johnson's Health & Wellness programs. There are also reduced insurance claims, disability days and rehabilitation costs. While no accurate measurements exist, the company is confident that the health culture has also increased productivity, improved morale and impacted performance.

Future focus

The improving health of Johnson & Johnson employees is spreading beyond employees and their families to the surrounding communities through various health literacy initiatives that educate and serve. The Caregiver Initiative helps those caring for loved ones. There are several community outreach programs that promote prevention and disease management, encourage early care and teach people how to seek out and assess health information. All of these are ways to improve the health literacy of at-risk populations.

Johnson & Johnson also articulates ideas for other employer led, evidence-based health and well-being programs via our chairmanship of the World Economic Forum's Working Toward Wellness Project Board and our ongoing leadership role within Partnership for Prevention in the United States. We also join with other multinational corporations in an effort to reduce our "environmental footprint" through reduced paper use, reduced emissions and so on. Similarly the company strives to expand its "health footprint" by addressing the health and well-being of the population beyond its site walls.

While continuing to focus on the four target areas of inactivity, hypertension, cholesterol and tobacco use, Johnson & Johnson has set goals for 2015 to ensure their *Healthy People* programs are optimally utilized. The goals include:

- 90 percent of employees having access to culture of health programs
- 80 percent of employees having completed a health risk profile and know their key health indicators
- At least 80 percent of employees characterized as "low health risk" (0–2 risk factors).

In addition to the above goals, Johnson & Johnson seeks to improve its ability to measure and improve employee performance and engagement, mental health and stress trends, diabetes risk, health literacy, and absenteeism and presenteeism. With the excellent base of information the company has, it plans to continue gathering data over time for a more longitudinal perspective on the influence of health risk changes on employee satisfaction, medical care costs and company profitability.

CHAPTER 12

ENGAGING IN HEALTH AND WELL-BEING

Jessica Colling
vielife[1]

BACKGROUND

Whilst the case may be strong for the role of well-being in personal happiness and for increased productivity, the challenge faced by many organizations and health promoters is how to get people engaged in health and well-being. Sadly, many people only engage in their health once things start to go wrong; yet, there is extensive evidence[2, 3, 4] that a healthy lifestyle can increase life expectancy and substantially reduce the risks of a raft of medical conditions.

So, how do you get people to participate in well-being programs in the workplace? This case study describes how at vielife we have spent a considerable amount of time creating well-being solutions and tailoring campaigns for organizations and have identified key components that can help predict the success of a particular campaign.

BOX 12.1 **Golden rules of engagement**

The golden rules of engagement:

- Make it relevant to your workforce
- Use a variety of communication channels

BOX 12.1 **(Continued)**

- Make it visually compelling
- Keep it simple
- Make it culturally appropriate
- Incentivize appropriately
- Have clear and vocal management support
- Use internal champions to be ambassadors of the initiative
- Be flexible – be prepared to adapt the solution based on feedback and experience

---

THE APPROACH

Planning

Planning won't necessarily determine the success of your program; however, it will help you avoid major pitfalls and measure if you've achieved the success that you wanted. It will also help you identify if your goals are realistic.

Key areas for consideration

It's very important in any well-being project to be clear about the objective. Why is your company investing in a well-being program and what do you hope to get from it? Once you know why and what, the question is then, how are you going to measure if you have been successful?

Identifying what resources you have available is also critical. Interestingly, one of the key factors in a successful program isn't overall budget; it is the availability of people to work on the project and in getting internal support and buy in. Spending time up front getting all the internal teams bought in to the project, having a senior sponsor who really carries weight in the organization and who is prepared to be an advocate are significantly more important in driving engagement and success than a multi-million dollar budget. Clearly, having a financial budget is essential, but the size of the number alone doesn't determine success.

Once the project goals and resources are clear there are a number of other practical considerations that can affect the success of the initiative.

- **Think about the right time to launch the initiative.** Are there any natural windows of opportunity to launch, for example, the New Year, or Easter-time for a pre-summer health kick, or September to coincide with a new school year? Are there any black spots in the year to avoid, for example, popular holiday times or the financial end of year?
- **Line up internal resources.** How much lead time do you need to build in to get materials created, solutions designed and approval given?
- **How long do you want the campaign to last?** A particular length of time or is this part of a long-term commitment to overall organization culture?

Designing an engaging solution

To be engaging, you need to understand your audience. What is important to them? What do you know about what they are interested in? Try to spend some time gathering information through focus groups or explore ideas with management and key opinion formers.

There are lots of ways of tackling health and well-being in the workplace and there is no one-size-fits-all solution. What will work for you depends on the kind of workplace you have: one central office, dispersed office locations, manufacturing environment, retail outlets, call centers, home workers, mobile offices, warehousing or a combination of any of the above, and also what kind of culture you have. It is important that the communications and solution that you offer take account of the ways people will interact with the program. For example, in an office environment an online solution with some physical on-site launch event may be the ideal solution; however, in a manufacturing environment or warehouse where people don't have frequent access to a computer, a combination of printed materials and on-site activities may be more appropriate. Equally, in a call center, where computers are available but external Internet access is limited and working time is precisely controlled, arrangements with line managers for enabling people to have time and access to participate is essential for engagement to happen.

Communication channels

Think about the communication media available to you: email, face-to-face, printed materials, text messaging, phone, voicemail, pay check messages, Intranet, induction packs. Which ones work best for your organization as a whole, and for the individual parts of your organization? Is there anything that is really off-limits? Try to use as many different channels as possible to get your message out; don't just rely on posters and emails! Messages and communication channels that are different to the norm get people's attention.

Look and feel

This leads on to the question of branding. Do you want your solution to look like a seamless part of your corporate brand, or do you want something different? Are you looking to realize a look and feel that belongs to your organization or are you wanting to bring in a partner to deliver the solution and make it clear that it is from outside? There is no "right answer" to this question: only what is right for your organization. Indeed, in our experience, which way you choose to go is not the strongest determinant of the success of the program. Making sure that it looks appealing is, however, a key factor in driving initial engagement.

One thing that is important to address no matter what the brand is confidentiality. Be up front about who has access to information that people provide, be it answers to assessments and questionnaires, or attendance at seminars. In our experience, when individuals see that personal health information may be going back to their employer this can be a deal breaker and cause a dramatic reduction in participation. Trust is key and to have trust requires openness; if other people in the organization will have access to an individual's information, be clear about how the information will be used.

Engagement starts from the very first communications about an initiative so it is worth spending time thinking about the right design and messaging for your population. You can have the most interesting, informative and engaging text in the world, but if the materials don't look appealing, people won't pick them up to read the text. Think about the images that would work for your population – one size doesn't have to fit all. By using different themes you can tailor your program so that you address people's particular desires without having to run completely different projects on different sites. This is essential if the program is to be cost-effective.

Cultural relevance

Another element in the design is making sure that it is culturally relevant. If you are rolling out a solution in many different global locations, getting the imagery and look and feel right across these territories is essential for engaging people.

This also applies to the text within materials. Referencing food types or activities that are not usual in a particular country stops the information being relevant, and that stops people engaging. For example, tailoring a UK product for Dubai means watching out for outdoor activity references such as "walking round the block" and making sure that examples that involve being outside in a near $40°C$ heat are not used. This is in addition to addressing local spellings and using appropriate references to support the information or recommendations, as well as any language translation that may be necessary.

To be engaging, a solution has to be relevant to the person receiving it. It doesn't matter what the mode of communication is or where in the world someone is, it's important to make it clear how this program will affect them and why they should take part.

Keep it simple

Make it easy for people to access and take part. As soon as people have to make an effort to participate or wait for something to happen, engagement starts to drop off. One such example of this is around registration and password setting for online health assessment participation. In vielife's first online health platform built in 2001 it was necessary to wait for an automated password link to be sent by email to a participant when they had registered with the site. This meant that there was the potential for the email to get trapped in a spam filter, or on occasions for the email to take many minutes to arrive and for the participant became tired of waiting. Both events made for an unnecessary drop off between people registering for the site and actually participating in the health assessments. Technology improvements meant that on the next generation of the platform this was not the case: participants set their password as they entered the site and could move straight into the online activities. This has resulted in a conversion rate of over 90 percent between registrations and health assessment completions. Taking out a potential blocker didn't affect the number of people who wanted to take part, but it meant that nearly all those who wanted to get involved ended up doing so.

Another key feature is clarity: less is more. You may need to repeat your message many times in different ways to reach the audience you want: "Why do they need it?" and "How do they get involved?".

Other ways of making things easy include using existing communication channels: how do people expect to get information about new initiatives in the company? Use materials people will take home, like pay slips, hold on-site events in highly visible places which have a high natural footfall. Put posters in private areas to jot down access information for services like Employee Assistance Programmes, Stress Lines or Health Coaching. Make information freely available and widely distributed.

Motivation

Incentives can be very effective at driving participation in a particular event or activity. If a high level of participation is a key success factor, using an incentive may be something worth considering. Incentives can take many forms from a simple prize draw to a financial incentive (or penalty) linked to other employee benefits. How much you want or need to incentivize depends on a number of things, including cultural expectations around incentives and their value; for example, in the United States where incentives are a common part of health program design, employees are frequently offered $100+ to complete a health risk assessment. This kind of value incentive is highly unlikely in Europe due to the difference in the way that health care is funded.

However, in Europe, we have seen organizations offer participants a reduction in their health insurance excess, rather than a gift card or cash bonus. One particular client that made these changes to their insurance excess achieves participation in the region of 90 percent on an annual basis. (Interestingly, before linking participation to an incentive this client was able to achieve around 70 percent participation through strong leadership and advocacy of the program).

More frequently in Europe a prize draw is used as an incentive for participation. Prizes usually range from mountain bikes and spa days to additional days' vacation time. The value or number of the incentives needs to be proportional to the likelihood of winning. In a small office, a £50 voucher may be sufficient to drive participation; in a large multi-national, where the chances of winning are significantly lower, the prize pot may need to be worth thousands, for example, exclusive holiday, car, lottery-style cash draw or lots of small prizes on offer. Good practice would also suggest that prize incentives are relevant to achieving or keeping a healthy lifestyle.

There is research to support the use of incentives in driving engagement; however, their efficacy in creating long-term health improvements is much less clear. Incentives appear to need to be time-boxed so that they have the desired effect and if they are for changes in behavior, staggering the reward seems to have the biggest impact. Making sure these are awarded quickly after the activity is also beneficial to maintain momentum.

Championing the cause

Getting buy in from all levels in the organization is important for a successful health improvement program. Ideally a vocal and well-respected senior executive will champion the program from the top, but getting the buy in of line managers and local champions is just as important, sometimes even more so.

Local champions

One thing that has been very successful in driving engagement in health and well-being programs is to have internal advocates from all levels of the organization who can champion participation. Using natural opinion formers and leaders to drive this, and providing training and incentives to get involved can be a very cost-effective engagement tool. Interestingly, we have found that the visibility of being a champion and tying this to performance objectives can be important. Also, having incentives that are not "for sale", for example, an additional day's holiday, or recognition within the organization, have been more effective at motivating people to champion the program than items that they could buy for themselves. Ideal champions are people who are natural leaders with a strong interest in health and well-being, who have excellent communication skills, organizational ability and access to email.

Champions are also highly valuable for gathering feedback about the solution that you are offering. If you want to know which pieces could be enhanced, the champions are a mine of information. They also provide continuity and ongoing support for a program that may have a number of different elements throughout the year.

OUTCOMES AND EVALUATION

Having variety in your solution will help you reach the maximum number of people. You can have core central parts, but giving people choice around what they participate in is also important. Technology has enabled huge flexibility in the solutions that can be provided and allows different information to be surfaced to different people. This can take the form of a questionnaire or assessment and the provision of a personalized report, segmentation of email communications based on particular profile or health status, text message alerts based on preferences or changes in imagery depending on the age and gender of the participant, to name but a few, ever-expanding, possibilities. Making sure that you can tailor the solution for individuals and different parts of your organization is important. As addressed earlier, one size often doesn't fit all even within the same organization.

If you don't know exactly what you want your health and well-being program to look like and want to make sure you use your budget in the most effective area, an assessment or questionnaire can be a useful first step in your initiative. This can help identify which areas need most attention and where you can get the best return on investment.

It's also important to remember that you don't need to launch all initiatives at the same time. Being able to drip feed the program will help it stay fresh and provide a continual engagement drive. This strategy also builds in a key feature: that of flexibility. Being able to move campaigns and respond to feedback allows a high degree of agility, the opportunity to really tailor a solution to the organization, and provides the ability to take advantage of new technologies and information.

The key to engagement is about knowing your audience and being able to respond to them in a way that lets them know you've been listening. (Boxes 12.2 and 12.3 show case studies of initiatives that have worked well. Box 12.4 shows themes when engagement hasn't been so successful.)

BOX 12.2   **Case study: Standard Life Health care**

2002 – 72 percent engagement
2009 – 90 percent engagement

Engagement strategies

- Management endorsement
- Champion network
- Incentives – prize draw, free fruit, reduction in PMI excess
- Posters
- Emails
- Handouts
- Research project

BOX 12.3   **Case study: Severn Trent Water**

60 percent engagement

Engagement strategies

- Management endorsement
- Champion network
- Incentives – prize draw, water bottle
- "Harmony" "branded-health & well-being" strategy
- Paper and online health assessment
- Posters and handouts
- Emails
- Handouts
- Award recognition

BOX 12.4   **When it hasn't worked** . . .

- Lack of management support
- Poor organizational support
- Lack of resource
- Poor messaging
- Poor communication
- Internal restructuring

CHAPTER 13

THE DEVELOPMENT OF A COMPREHENSIVE CORPORATE HEALTH MANAGEMENT SYSTEM FOR WELL-BEING

Karl Kuhn and Klaus Pelster
Germany

OVERVIEW

This case study describes the process of introducing and sustaining a comprehensive corporate health management system in a company in the chemical industry.

The company, Evonik Degussa GmbH, is an international industrial group operating within the Chemical, Energy and Real Estate sectors. The starting point for the intervention was the setting up of an interdisciplinary steering group for the management, the implementation of measures and for the evaluation of the whole process. Besides the top management of the company, representatives of HR (human resources), OSH (occupational safety and health), OD (organizational development), the works council and different production departments were all involved in the steering group. The Chairperson of the steering group was a representative of occupational medicine (medical service). The steering group was supported permanently by external representatives of two different statutory health insurers. During the past 15 years, this steering group initiated a great many projects promoting and enabling the health, engagement and well-being of employees. The activities focused on the prevention of musculo-skeletal disorders, lifestyle changes and the promotion of strategies for coping with an ageing workforce. This case study deals with the problem of how all the implemented measures can be sustained, and how the activities can be implemented within the structures and pro-cesses of the enterprise. The case study could be used as a blueprint for other companies on how well-being initiatives can be integrated in continuous action-orientated projects.

According to the German Social Code V §20 health promotion activ-ities are an obligation for health insurance funds in Germany. They have the opportunity to invest in, and influence, health promotion activities. In 2000, the Associations of Health Insurance Funds devel-oped quality guidelines for workplace health promotion, which were modified and enlarged during the following years. These guidelines assure quality management of health promotion activities, documen-tation of all activities in this field and proper and systematic eval-uation. There are clear guidelines for the qualification of providers of health promotion activities. There is a difference between indi-vidual approaches to change behavior (physical activity, nutrition, stress reduction, drug abuse, etc.) and building organizational change in a variety of settings (i.e. for schools, municipalities/local activ-ities, companies and workplaces). The AOK Rhinland, a regional health insurance in Northshine-Westfalia, has its own institute (BGF Institut) for workplace health promotion, with experts in various fields to support enterprises in undertaking health promotion activi-ties. This Institute was actively involved in the case study described below.

BACKGROUND

The present case study is based on a company employing approx-imately 350 employees, which is part of the international global company. The average age of the workforce has increased during the past few years, with currently a mean age of over 45. Apart from a small fluctuation, the reason for this development lies particularly in restrictive recruitment practices. The number of people employed sank in the past 15 years from about 700 to 350 today. This decline was managed primarily through natural wastage and retirement.

THE APPROACH

In the context of a first restructuring wave in the early 90s, a campaign for lifelong learning was started. A requirement for continued employment within the enterprise was a request to all employees to achieve at least one further vocational skill certified by the Chamber of Commerce (IHK). Because this demand applied to the long-term employed and middle-aged workers, it was a major challenge, in particular for the older workforce. The campaign currently comprises four components:

1. Seminars for employees (all age groups) to support lifelong learning; employees have to contribute two-thirds of the learning time, non-paid from their own leisure time, one-third from the company's time.
2. About 20 computerized self-learning programs for home use offer information on various topics, which may be professionally relevant but there are others which help self-development.
3. "On-the-job training" designed to increase company-related skills and competences.
4. To preserve the employability of the employees during phases of restructuring, new training and qualifications are offered.

The result of this campaign was:

- Greater individual responsibility and initiative from employees in relation to their skills and employability
- Increased commitment of workers over 50 years of age
- Increased participation in training and learning programs

Besides the production function, there is an R&D function in this particular company. The majority of the people employed are working in three-shift systems. During the period of the intervention, an integrated management system, which united the topic fields of the environment, health and safety and quality management with one another, was introduced. A further challenge was the area-wide introduction of group work, with the goal to develop the organization into a "learning organization". Each group as a whole had responsibility for achieving the final aims and objectives of the production task. Thereby, more and more responsibility was given to the groups and to the individual workers. Apart from operational planning, these groups were responsible for the continuous improvement of the production process. To achieve this, regular group sessions were organized. When required in-house experts from different areas could be consulted.

The purpose and goals interventions

The stimulus for the introduction of a health management system came from close co-operation with the compulsory health insurance Rhineland in the early 90s. As mentioned earlier, the health insurance Rhineland (AOK Rheinland) offered workplace health promotion as part of their portfolio. These services were predominantly offered to medium-sized enterprises.

In the case study company, this offer was seen as a useful supplement at that time, as the company was already intensively pursuing activities in the field of OSH and health promotion. It took place under the activity portfolio of the steering group called "healthy work", which still exists today, despite the changing composition of the group. The management of this steering group was the responsibility of the occupational medical service of the enterprise. The permanent participation of the top management in all meetings is seen as an important criterion for success in relation to the effectiveness and efficiency of the steering group. Since its establishment, a representative of the employee works council also participated in the working group. Through this representation, a balance between the various industrial relations interests was ensured and proper communications undertaken to all employees. In the course of these activities, various action areas were developed, of which the following three will be described in more detail. These three activities are currently still ongoing.

1. The prevention of musculoskeletal disorders
2. The improvement of nutrition habits
3. And, the management of demographic change.

Activities for the prevention of musculoskeletal disorders

At the same time as the start of the activities of the steering group "healthy work" in the 90s, the implementation of the obligatory risk assessment was installed by the representatives of the health and safety committee. A substantial analysis of the risk situation in the enterprise was thereby created. This legally, obligatory health risk assessment was supplemented by an analysis of the ergonomics of the work. Bringing both results together, a catalogue of measures was developed with concrete proposals for changing the workplace layout and the organization of work. Further outcomes included suggestions for training in "move-well behaviours" on the job, that is, how to prevent accidents and musculoskeletal problems. Additionally, the urgent need for interventions in this area became apparent through the analysis of the aggregated sick-leave data of the company, which showed above-average prevalence of musculoskeletal disorders in the workforce. Both behavior-orientated and condition-orientated interventions were implemented from there on. The updating of the risk assessment has been transferred into the everyday operational routines of the enterprise in the meantime.

After the training courses in "move-fair behaviours", two training offers were permanently installed in order to provide sustainability: (1) every month a back exercise course including balance, stretching and strengthening exercises is offered in a break area; (2) practical tips and tricks regarding positioning during working time are also included in the program. Additionally a massage is offered by a qualified masseur. The appointments for this service are made by the medical service in the enterprise. The enterprise provides these services on site. The time for the massage is during non-paid working time. For the sustaining of the training course modules, information meetings were developed and organized in the context of the integrated management system. At present, the integration of this program into the groupwork on the production line has taken place. To raise awareness of the workforce on these training programs, trunk musculature tests by means of "back checks" were organized. The results of these are discussed in the workgroup more generally. Together with a trained posture and orthopaedic health professional, the workgroup discusses the specific work characteristics and the occurrence of load factors on the muscle and skeletal system. Out of these discussions, process improvement measures have been developed and, whenever possible, directly implemented. The satisfaction with the interventions is evaluated by surveys and by analysis of the routine data concerning health insurances (sick-leave by diagnostic group). The results show that despite the rising average age of the workforce, no increase of musculoskeletal disorders has been observed. This was a positive benchmark! Nowadays, back health is integrated into the management system, in the continuous improvement process of the enterprise, and all groups in the enterprise have been tasked to develop at least one proposal for the prevention of musculoskeletal disorders.

Activities for the improvement of employee nutrition

Another health and safety intervention was to improve the nutrition of the employees of the enterprise. The reason for this was the identification of increasing problems among employees of nutrition-related diseases. At the same time evaluations of the PROCAM Score (an indicator of the risk of heart disease) showed extreme values. Furthermore, in-house surveys showed high dissatisfaction with the canteen food. The health promotion steering group took up this issue. To raise awareness about eating habits, special information and screenings were offered. Together with experts from the health insurers, representatives of the occupational medical service organized special "health days" in the cafeteria/canteen. In addition to the measurement of blood pressure, body weight and "hip to waist ratio", a drive was on to change the nutritional behavior of the employees. Every day was a particular health day, with a motto such as "a healthy heart" day or "a five a day" day! The challenge here was the integration of the canteen, which is operated by an external caterer. From time to time tension arose over discussion about the menus during the health actions (e.g., during the action on a "healthy heart" – no fatty meals), and, on the other hand, efforts to bring about improvements in the preparation of the meals. In the meantime, the food preparation could very clearly be improved by regular cafeteria audits.

As concrete measures, courses were implemented for healthy eating habits. Also a combination of exercise and nutrition was conducted by experts from the health insurance organization. With diaries for nutrition and exercise the individual development of each participant was pursued. Recipes and advice for taking exercise ensured that the social environment outside of work was included. Group courses in the company increased the team spirit and offered the opportunity to learn new information. To ensure sustainability, regular cafeteria audits, the health checks offered by the medical service as well as nutrition counseling in the enterprise are important. There are plans for this counseling to be further developed to offer individual solutions for nutrition-related disorders.

The costs are covered by health insurance; the recommendation for participation is given by the medical service.

Management of the demographic change

As already described, the age structure in the enterprise is rising continuously. New appointments of younger people have not been made and retiring workers usually have not been replaced. The collective agreement in the chemical industry in Germany "Work in life course and Demography" obliges the industry to evaluate the age structure of the company. This is done through the age-structure analysis tool (a tool that is used widely in Germany). Based on this evaluation and on the observation of the future development of the age structure in the enterprise, the steering group "healthy work" set the topic ageing in the enterprise on its agenda. The first step in this action field was to raise the awareness of the workforce. For this reason a 15-minute film was produced under the title *For healthy ageing you have to start at the beginning!* Scenes from the company and statements of people employed are included in the film. With this film an internal discussion process was started to sensitize the workers and managers to the coming challenge of an ageing workforce. For the development of concrete measures in this area again the participative approach via the group work was chosen. The film was shown to the work groups and in a follow-up meeting the topic was discussed under the questions, "What do I have to do to go healthily into retirement?" and "What does the enterprise have to do so I can go healthily into retirement?"

In the meantime more than 40 group meetings and more than 500 proposals were compiled. In these proposals emphasis lay on nutrition (28 percent of all proposals), sports and exercise (25 percent), personal development (17 percent), organizational change (17 percent) and communication and information (17 percent). The compilation and prioritization provided a master list, which was further processed in the steering group. Continuous communication about the implementation provided clear transparency of the procedure. This process is ongoing.

OUTCOMES AND EVALUATION

Due to the multiplicity of different activities a comprehensive evaluation of the last 15 years is difficult. Some of the evaluation tools have already been described. One result can be shown through the sickness-absence rates of the enterprise using data from health insurance. This data are analyzed in relation to diagnostic groups in an aggregated manner and always delivered to the company annually in the form of a company health report. Despite the rising average age, the sick-leave rates have remained constant for years and are below the rates of other enterprises in the chemical industry. This may be seen as an indication that investments in human resources are worthwhile themselves and cost-effective. The value placed on these activities by the company is supported by the fact that, even against the background of continuous restructuring and an associated staff reduction, the activities in the field of workplace health promotion were not cut back. In conclusion relevant success factors are:

- A sophisticated plan for the establishment of lifelong learning-programs in the awareness of employees
- Focused cooperation between staff, the people responsible for the program implementation, the works council and the steering group
- Financing of most of the program by the company
- Simple registration and participation
- Thorough planning and organization

CHAPTER 14

THE JOURNEY TOWARD ORGANIZATIONAL RESILIENCE AT THE UNIVERSITY OF LEEDS

Nina Quinlan and Gary Tideswell
University of Leeds, Wellbeing Safety & Health

OVERVIEW

This case study presents one higher education institution's (HEI's) ongoing journey over a 10-year timeline, which began, in 2005, with the need to improve health and safety management, and evolved, by 2010, to integrate well-being and the ethos of a "Well University", based on a holistic settings approach. We present an incomplete journey, moving toward building organizational resilience by 2015, and take readers through the thinking that influenced and shaped the well-being direction and some of the subsequent actions that were taken.

BACKGROUND

The University of Leeds in England employs around 7500 staff, and has a student population of 50,000. At the start of the well-being journey in 2005, we had identified a significant number of health, safety and well-being issues that raised questions about our ability to offer a safe and healthy working environment, and to maintain our reputation as a leading UK university.

In summary, these were an immediate need to improve health and safety management across campus, strengthened by Health and Safety Executive scrutiny and improvement notices, with a key issue being work-related stress. In addition, our staff population was fairly stable with low staff turnover, particularly for academic and professional staff groups. This stability, whilst giving an indication of staff satis-faction with the University as an employer, meant the average age of staff members was increasing, with subsequent increases in risk from age-related health conditions. However, support for health risk man-agement was inconsistent and did not place us in a strong position to control health risks.

Also, in 2005, two other considerations came together which led to an increase in the pace of change. Firstly, there was a growing real-ization that there was a mismatch between the University's potential, such as its research excellence and its high quality of staff, and its standing amongst other Universities – globally and nationally. There was a general feeling that we were "punching below our weight" when national and global university rankings were published and these rank-ings were becoming increasingly important in a growing global market for the best academic staff and the best students who could continue to build on the reputation and standing of the University.

Secondly, the University had evidenced, through reaction to exter-nal pressures, that our organizational resilience was not very robust.

These challenges created a need to review our strategic direction in relation to our vision and goals, including consideration of the organizational development agenda.

Fortunately, at this time, there was a huge opportunity offered by the appointment of a new vice chancellor and the subsequent devel-opment of a new strategic plan and vision, which recognized the value of the people who make up the University community and explicitly placed this very high on the agenda for improvement. This created the potential for a dual approach which could integrate prin-ciples of health improvement along with organizational development to achieve the overall strategic goal of improved performance.

THE APPROACH

Preparing the ground

There were three preparatory stages in moving the University toward a more health and well-being supportive environment:

- identifying the theoretical approach that would underpin and be integrated into all subsequent activities

- recruiting the right staff with the right skills who could deliver against the issues
- engaging our people to inform the prioritization of activities and define the overall outcomes and goals.

Theoretical approach

The approach taken was based on a broader concept of "public health" which viewed the University as a "setting" which could provide an opportunity for health and well-being improvements. A "healthy setting" was first articulated in the Ottawa Charter (WHO, 1988) and provided a fairly simplistic model of how to create a setting which integrates health improvement activities into its structures, policies, process and procedures, with the intended outcome of improved health of everyone within the setting. With use however, the idea of a setting has evolved into something more holistic which appreciates that a more realistic understanding of the complexity of an organization, grounded in organizational, systems and management theory, is more successful at creating healthy settings (Dooris, 2001; Paton et al., 2005), but still creates difficulties evidencing improvement (Dooris and Doherty, 2010). This does create a challenge however, as organizational management theory does not explicitly place health and well-being at the center of its agenda.

At the University, this challenge presented itself as a dichotomy between the desire to improve the health and well-being of our staff and students, and a recognition and belief in the need to look beyond health, toward factors which contribute toward well-being at work, including leadership and management practices, structures and processes, and implicit and explicit cultures within the institution. This resulted in the University broadening the concept of a "Health Promoting University", into an idea and model of a "Well University" which looks beyond health improvement and aims to achieve sustainable and tangible, practical, structural and cultural changes which will enable the delivery of improved organizational performance.

Other drivers were also reinforcing the relationships between a broader holistic settings approach and improved organizational performance. The first of these was the University's drive toward achieving the "Investors in People" leadership and management standard, with a whole range of activities aiming to improve the way our

159

leaders lead and manage being introduced. Additionally, activities aiming to build a sense of engagement and ownership of our university values were being initiated and were attracting "pump prime" funding. In addition, from an external perspective, educational institutions were increasingly being cited in government guidelines as relevant settings for creating opportunities for health (DoH, 2004).

Finally, the University's organizational structure combined monocratic decision-making based on a traditional hierarchical structure, with decisions being made at "the top" and cascading down, with heterocratic structures whereby decentralized authority supports rational decision-making routines and processes (Morrill et al., 1999), and this enabled us to embed the theoretical model into subsequent activities and gave freedom for innovative practical implementation and delivery.

Having the right people in place

Delivering these changes needed the right staff. In this, the University was innovative and open to ideas, which led to the creation of two new roles. Firstly, a role for the United Kingdom's first Higher Education (HE) Director of Wellbeing, Safety and Health, which reflected the urgency of resolving the immediate health and safety issues, but offered the opportunity to broaden the role to encompass well-being. This was a significant departure from traditional health and safety management and created the platform to move away from the reductionist model of health, as meaning "ill health", toward improving positive well-being. In support, an additional role of Wellbeing Project Manager was created, which specifically highlighted the importance of understanding the "settings based approach" as a guide toward practical ways of improving the well-being at the University. The dedicated role ensured that multi-level activities could be co-ordinated and implemented, including policy development, practical health improvement and health promotion, staff engagement activities, improvement of structures, development and delivery of training, creation of supportive networks, sharing learning across the HE sector and innovative, "fun" activities.

To enable changes to be made, the well-being staff were located within a department that cut across both staff and student groups, and this created greater opportunities to influence health and well-being across the institution.

Engaging our people

Following this, a period of time was spent developing engagement in "well-being" as a concept, and consultation to identify and agree a series of "well-being principles" within which activities could be mapped, and against which improvement could be monitored. This was achieved through three means.

Firstly, to gain buy in to the idea of a "Well University", an "information gathering" process was carried out with staff and students representing all the major employment groups, the campus trade unions and student bodies. Through formal structured meetings, informal discussions, question and answer sessions and focus groups, a perspective on existing understanding of well-being meanings and priorities was gained. When compared with the more theoretical concept of organizational well-being, this enabled the size and scope of the well-being journey to be fully understood.

This was followed up with a formal "focus group" consultation where participants identified what "organizational well-being" could look like, and led to the creation of a series of "well-being principles". Finally, to bring this together into a coherent structure that could be communicated effectively, a "well-being brand" was created which tied together the "well-being principles", mapped this against existing well-being support, and enabled identification of gaps which could then form action priorities.

Practical implementation

In planning and delivering activities, three core principles underpinned our choice of activity and our methods used. These were

- To evaluate as rigorously as possible to show the benefits of the activity. This was important internally to ensure continued support for well-being within the University, and also to engage our academic community, some of whom were critical of well-being due to the lack of supporting evidence. Externally, the evidence

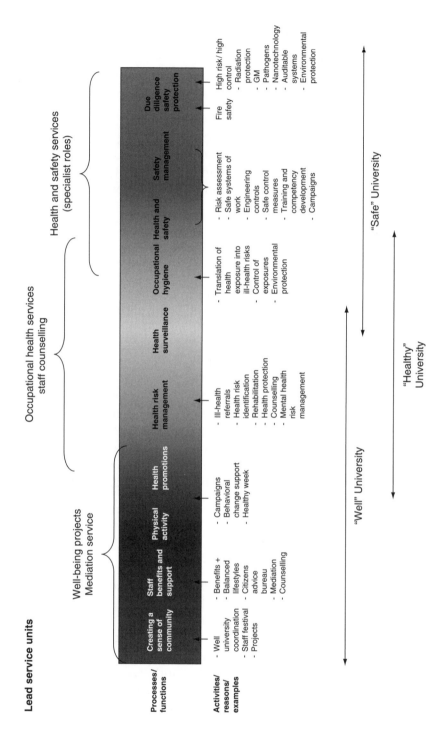

FIGURE 14.1 **Toward organizational well-being – a continuum of activities**©

Note: © Gary Tideswell.

162

base supporting well-being activities was being recognized as lacking (DWP and DoH, 2008), and a broader range of methods showing evidence of benefit was called for by NICE (2009).

- To ensure our activities were located within a well-being strategic framework which showed how the activities and projects that were taking place were aligned with the overall institutional vision. Figure 14.1 – the well-being continuum sets out our model of the processes and functions needed to deliver on our definition of "organizational well-being", and attributes activities and lead areas responsible. The model located activities from extreme compliance at one end, to the fun, engagement activities at the other.
- To look for opportunities to broaden the impact of well-being activities by considering all aspects of the environment, as defined in a settings approach to improving health and well-being.

Since 2007, activities to build our resilience and develop organizational well-being have included fun projects such as the delivery of an annual "staff festival" as a way of showing how we value our staff, and a 12-week collaborative project with the Flower Council of Holland to explore the impact of flowers in communal work spaces; health improvement projects such as an award-winning six-month on-line health risk management pilot which demonstrated a clear return on investment; through to more serious activities such as an award-winning health and safety campaign promoting individual knowledge, awareness and responsibility for health and safety.

The two examples presented below give a little more detail for readers about two particular projects, and include a brief description of the activity, what the impact was, and picks up on how these three core principles were integrated (see Boxes 14.1 and 14.2).

BOX 14.1   **Using staff survey findings to build organizational resilience – how "improving stress management" evolved into "creating a culture of dignity and mutual respect"**

In 2008, although annual staff surveys had been carried out over a 4-year period, response rates were decreasing year on year, with feedback showing a lack of ownership of the survey process and results; inefficient communications linking results to actions taken; and academic critique of the validity of

---

BOX 14.1 **(Continued)**

surveys with low response rates. Alongside this, the University was charged by the Health and Safety Executive to improve the way it monitored and managed work-related stressors. This created an opportunity to carry out a staff survey which engaged staff more effectively and also supported a process which improved the management of work-related stressors.

Extensive consultation at all levels informed the design and agreement of the survey questions, delivery mechanism and follow-up response planning. Then, following targeted communications to engage staff at every level, a university wide staff survey was delivered in the spring of 2008. Survey delivery and promotion was based on local management team ownership and management buy in was helped by being brutally honest about the strengths and limitations of the survey tool, as well as showing flexibility in accommodating suggestions from managers as they arose. A multi-disciplinary team supported every management area, ensuring that issues could be rapidly responded to by somebody with relevant expertise. To ensure that institutional actions could also be implemented, a follow-up process was planned by a working group including members of the University Executive Group, directorate and campus trade unions.

This approach saw a dramatic increase in response rates – from 23 percent to 53 percent. Particular successes for ancillary staff, who find it difficult to access online surveys, saw response rates rise from 4 percent to 44 percent. Embedding principles of effective public health based on taking the support to where and when staff can access them was adopted and embraced by the ancillary staff management team. The survey results led to a range of interventions responding to concerns about bullying, harassment and to the building of positive working relationships. These included:

- Creating a relationships group in one work area to explore positive working relationships, and map this against staff experiences. Gaps identified were communicated and a staff suggestions box gathered ideas for addressing the gaps. The eventual actions taken were those voted by staff as most likely to address the gaps identified.
- Developing a policy on dignity and mutual respect to replace the 'Code of Conduct on Bullying and Harassment'. This policy placed a positive emphasis on desirable behaviors but also provided clear signposting and timescales for action should behavior fall short of the stated standards.
- Developing and delivering an intervention where there were clear issues around respect, using externally facilitated focus groups to explore a range of themes with staff and producing a series of recommendations.
- Integrating stressor management into regular meeting and monitoring processes, at each individual management team level.

BOX 14.2 **Using executive coaching to build personal resilience during challenging times**

We piloted a program of individual executive coaching, offered to pre-selected senior managers in a faculty which was in the middle of major structural review. Existing support was primarily formal support from Human Resources based on principles of organizational change. This intervention was developed to broaden the support and to evaluate the impact of a more personalized program.

Senior managers were offered four one-to-one sessions. The Executive Coach was specifically selected as external to the University as this offered the flexibility to discuss any issues that were relevant. The Executive Coach offered a wide toolkit of techniques, including Cognitive Behavioural Therapy (CBT), Neuro Linguistic Programming (NLP) and other techniques as this gave a range of options of coaching methodology. Three managers took up the coaching offer, and qualitative semi-structured interviews were carried out post coaching to evaluate the impact. The findings of the pilot showed that:

(a) Using an external coach was perceived to be hugely beneficial, giving managers the confidence to discuss issues without worrying that the Executive Coach had prior relationships or knowledge of that person.

(b) The combination of understanding of the HE setting along with broader expertise from across the public and private sector offered by the Coach was beneficial.

(c) The range of tools and methods offered enabled the coaching to respond to very particular issues, for example one participant reported sleeping better which, although not directly linked to improving management, helped the staff member to feel more able to meet the challenges of managing the changes.

(d) The coaching provided a variety of very specific practical tools and techniques that the managers were able to draw on in their day-to-day management, related to the breadth of approaches used in the coaching.

As a result of this pilot, the coaching offer has been extended to all senior executives responsible for managing structural change as a result of changing economic circumstances. A rigorous evaluation method, including qualitative and quantitative methods, as well as the inclusion of a control group will further build the evidence as to whether an individual approach improves resilience. The results of this more extensive intervention will be available in the summer of 2011.

OUTCOMES AND EVALUATION

Moving toward resilience

Coming toward the end of 2010, the groundwork that has been put in place to embed the idea of organizational resilience is beginning to make itself felt. The University has renewed its commitment to well-being and organizational resilience in its revised strategy and aims. However, at the time of writing, a new economic climate is beginning to make itself felt across the United Kingdom, with the challenge of "delivering more with less" alongside still creating a supportive and enabling working environment placing additional pressures on staff and on the achievement of organizational resilience. More recently, as the national economy contracts, moves to reduce costs associated with workplace ill-health frequently cite universities and large employers as having a unique responsibility and opportunity to improve workforce health (Black, 2008; DWP and DOH, 2009).

Taking all this into consideration, having put in place support structures to enable innovative work to improve well-being, the plan now is to further work to build resilience. Specifically, over the coming 5 years,

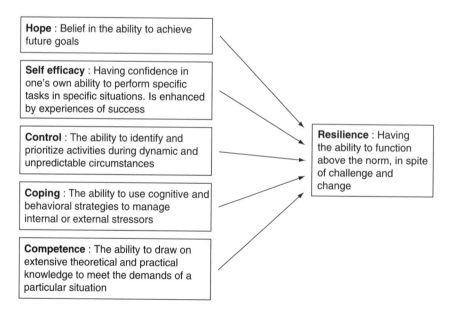

FIGURE 14.2 **Characteristics of resilience**

well-being activities will be directed toward developing individual resilience, defined as enabling our people to have the ability to function above the norm in spite of challenge and change (Gillespie et al., 2007), through building the particular characteristics of resilience as defined in research literature (Figure 14.2).

Our proposal is to focus on the creation of hope as a means of promoting resilience because, of all the above attributes, hope has the strongest correlation with resilience; integrates most of the other attributes; and is one area that is not being addressed through other work areas that has the potential to hugely improve our staff resilience.

Alongside this, organizational resilience will continue to be developed through robust evaluation of well-being activities, proactively anticipating and addressing support needs and, uniquely, learning from and sharing with our colleagues across the Higher Education sector. As part of this, Leeds are the lead partners in a cross-sectoral project to evidence the benefits of well-being in relation to performance, which has brought together institutions and funding from across England, Scotland and Wales.

CHAPTER 15

IMPROVING WELL-BEING AT LONDON FIRE BRIGADE

Mairin Finn
London Fire Brigade

and

Gordon Tinline
Robertson Cooper Ltd

OVERVIEW

BACKGROUND

The London Fire Brigade (LFB) is the largest fire and rescue service in the United Kingdom. It exists to make London a safer city. The organization's vision is to be a world-class fire and rescue service for London, Londoners and visitors. LFB employs approximately 7000 staff, of which 5800 are operational fire fighters and officers. It is part of a group of organizations under the "umbrella" of the Greater London Authority (GLA) and is the third largest fire-fighting organization in the world: protecting people and property from fire within the 1587 square kilometres of Greater London. Providing Londoners with 24/7 coverage, the LFB has 113 fire stations, plus the river station, which are crewed by four different watches, operating on a two-two-four watch system (two days on, two nights on, four days off). In meeting the needs of London, LFB is the only UK fire service to have a predominantly whole time (full-time) work force. Other brigades across the United Kingdom use a combination of full- and part-time staff, and "retained" fire fighters who carry out fire-fighting duties in addition to their usual employment.

THE APPROACH

In November 2005, LFB carried out a stress/well-being audit of all staff using Robertson Cooper's ASSET survey tool. ASSET is described in Chapter 5. The survey drew a 37 percent response from staff (N=2712). The results from the survey highlighted some positive findings relating to relationships at work and pride regarding the role of the organization. It also highlighted some hotspot areas, which indicated less than typical responses. In the main, these were perceived pressures about job security, change, resources, pay and benefits and control. Overall, the results were considered to be typical of an organization that was undergoing significant change, which since the 2003 industrial action that had taken place was very much the case at the LFB.

To further understand the results that had been achieved from the audit, a number of focus groups were run following the survey to help interpret the data and identify a range of possible solutions to the areas highlighted. These focus groups were then followed by a larger engagement exercise with line managers across the brigade, who were subsequently tasked with discussing further the results with their staff at fire stations. This was done to ensure that a full understanding of the results was gained and the outcomes of this work informed the development of corporate and departmental action plans. A stress steering group was set up, with all departments represented and overseen by a senior LFB manager. The group was tasked with monitoring and delivering both the corporate and departmental action plans.

As such, the stress/well-being audit served as a platform for the development and implementation of a wide range of new interventions which were driven by and included in the corporate action plan. This comprised four main streams of activity, which were considered to be key to addressing the areas identified: Communication; Change; Role Clarity; and Training. When developing the corporate action plan, a conscious decision was taken to utilize initiatives already being progressed by the organization. However, there were a number of specific interventions that were developed to address the gaps, where either the work being undertaken was not considered sufficient to address the issue(s) identified or where there were no specific work streams/packages planned that were considered to address that area (examples of which include the work around health and well-being, and some of the more specific training offerings developed).

The range of interventions included in LFB's corporate action plan are summarized below, and two of the most extensive programs of activity: the "Health Roadshows" – which focused on improving the general health and well-being of the workforce – and the "Fit for Life" training course – which sought to improve individuals personal resilience – are described more fully.

Interventions

- Communication – to further support communication in the organization, the results of the audit were widely communicated in internal bulletins, supported by a specific stress leaflet that explained the symptoms of stress and identified a range of available resources. In addition, as a result of a review of the organizations internal communications, a new approach and style was adopted for staff briefings and internal communications, which was further supported by the introduction of a new performance review system for staff.
- Change – work was undertaken to identify the behaviors required of managers to support change, and these were then reviewed as part of the range of development programs offered by LFB. A program of staff engagement "round table" discussions, developed to support any new change initiatives introduced, were utilized to provide feedback which was then incorporated into the planning and implementation process.
- Training – as part of a strategic review of training being undertaken by the training and development department, additional work was undertaken to understand and address any gaps in relation to the training activities delivered against the national Personal Qualities and Attributes (PQA) framework. This included work on developing a leadership strategy for the LFB, and reviewing the competencies and associated training requirement for effective Line Management. Further work included in this area was the development of specific offerings for individuals and managers around stress and well-being, with initiatives and an associated brand (LFB Healthy) being developed to support the improvement of the general well-being of the workforce.
- Role clarity – was supported by the development of a formal policy outlining the required elements for induction, the introduction of a

program of breakfast briefings for HQ-based staff. Improved role clarity was further supported by the introduction of a new performance review system (as mentioned above).

Health roadshows

The audit had highlighted that in some areas individuals' perceptions of their physical and psychological well-being were below average when compared to the general working population. As such, the LFB developed the "LFB Healthy" brand and associated strategy, under which a range of health and well-being promotional activities were undertaken.

This included the development of the LFB Healthy "Health Roadshows", which were high-impact events, delivered over 10 days, at a range of locations, in conjunction with the Brigade's occupational health provider. Staff from across LFB were invited to attend the events for up to an hour, where they could meet with health professionals and outside support organizations, to discuss a range of health topics (physical activity, pressure management, cancer awareness, healthy eating and so on) and have various health measures (height, weight, body mass index, hip to waste ratio, blood pressure, cholesterol, blood glucose, lung capacity, lung age and so on) taken.

Over 750 staff attended the events, of which over 400 of these were from fire stations. As a result of the events, a number of staff were either referred back to the occupational health provider, or the individual's GP for further monitoring. Thirty-six percent of those who attended the events indicated that they were going to change their lifestyle, with ninety-five percent of those who attended indicating that they would be interested in attending similar events in the future. As part of the evaluation process biometric data were also gathered, that enabled LFB to compare those who attended the events to the general population, and will provide data with which to benchmark the success of these events going forward.

Fit for life – personal resilience program

To further improve and support individuals who were experiencing high levels of pressure, the organization committed to deliver a personal resilience/stress reduction program. The "Fit for Life" course was a personal resilience program, which looked at pressures arising from both home and work. The six sessions were delivered incrementally as two-hour inputs over six weeks, with individuals required to complete homework in between the sessions. In this way the structure of the course supported and promoted a meaningful change in behavior and the acquisition of new skills.

The program was aligned to the cognitive behavioral therapy approach of stress reduction. The program covered: the physiology of stress; the identification of the individual symptoms of stress; the specifics of their personal stress cycle; through to the inclusion of their associated thoughts and behaviors; and finishing at session six with the identification of an individual personal resilience plan. An initial evaluation of this course found that individuals made significant improvements in both resilience and general well-being when comparing pre- and post-course self-ratings.

Overall the range of interventions by LFB adopted a combination of top-down (corporate/organizational) and bottom-up (individual centered) approaches, with a blend of focus on both physical health and fitness and psychological well-being. The positive impact of fitness and physical condition on psychological well-being is now well-established (e.g. Hayes and Ross, 1986; Fox, 1999; Hassmen et al., 2000; Penedo and Dahn, 2005).

Careful consideration was taken in the marketing of the various interventions, which sought to emphasize and draw on the positive outcomes of good mental well-being (namely resilience) and physical health rather than solely focussing on stress.

A range of different methods was considered to support the promotion of health and well-being in the organization, particularly in relation to overcoming the logistical challenges presented by the disparate nature of LFB's workforce. One alternative method piloted was utilizing well-being representatives/champions. However, feedback indicated that one well-being rep was required per watch (N = 456) for this to be a successful means of engaging all station-based staff fully. Co-ordinating and engaging with such a large number of individuals, whilst establishing the scope and purpose of LFB's health and well-being strategy, was not considered feasible in the initial stages of this program. It might however be something that is reconsidered once the brand and initial offerings are formally established and embedded.

OUTCOMES AND EVALUATION

The most important improvement for LFB attributed to the progressive introduction of new well-being initiatives has been a gradual, but ultimately substantial improvement in sickness-absence due to stress and mental health causes. At the time of the stress/well-being audit in 2005 Stress Anxiety/Depression (SAD) was the highest cause of sickness-absence, representing around 20 percent of the total. Four years later SAD was the sixth ranked cause of sickness-absence at eleven percent of all absence. This has been calculated as a direct saving to LFB of over £1.8 million.

As is often the case it is impossible to attribute the reduction in sickness-absence to any single intervention. However, there is little doubt that the range of interventions offered together with a strong integrated branding of well-being activity had delivered substantial benefits to the organization. As well as the headline sickness-absence improvement a number of other tangible benefits have been observed, which include an improved organizational awareness and understanding of "stress" – in terms of both its symptoms and the range of organizational resources on offer to support managers and individuals.

Looking back on the work undertaken in LFB, key lessons learnt were that the support and buy in of top managers was critical to the success of this project, as well as utilizing a combination of both top-down and bottom-up approaches to addressing stress and improving well-being in the workplace.

Key benefits of adopting this approach for the LFB were that the information generated from the Audit enabled the organization to prioritize issues, identifying only a small number of areas corporately that were not currently being addressed. More importantly conducting an audit enabled hotspots to be identified at a departmental level – where making small changes could really affect great change. In addition, through engaging managers in this process, LFB has raised the profile and awareness of stress and well-being, ultimately improving the organization's capacity to respond.

CHAPTER 16

ON THE USE OF INTERNET-DELIVERED INTERVENTIONS IN WORKSITE HEALTH PROMOTION

Rik Crutzen
CAPHRI
Maastricht University, The Netherlands

Nowadays, worksite health promotion interventions are increasingly being delivered through the Internet. Advantages of Internet-delivered interventions are – among other things – accessibility, anonymity and interactivity. Accessibility means that employees can use the intervention at their own convenience, 24/7, in the comfort of their own home or during lunch break at work. This is connected to the second advantage, anonymity. Use of Internet-delivered interventions can be completely anonymous, without colleagues knowing that the employee is, for example, stressed or wants to decrease his/her drinking behavior. If the employee has, for example, a shared office space or is not able to use the Internet-delivered intervention at work, the accessibility of the Internet makes it possible to use the intervention elsewhere (e.g., at home). Finally, through its interactive character, the Internet is an appropriate medium to deliver tailored health promotion interventions; interventions that offer only content that is relevant for the specific employee. The way in which this is usually done is by letting employees fill out a health risk assessment and subsequently offering intervention content that is related to the behaviors at risk and their related determinants.

An appropriate question to be asked is whether Internet-delivered interventions can be effective in promoting health. Numerous efficacy trials proved that Internet-delivered interventions can indeed be effective in promoting health, but that their usage is very low, especially when they are implemented for real (*in vivo*) rather than in a research setting (*in vitro*). For example, server statistics of an intervention promoting heart-healthy behaviors showed that 285,146 visitors from unique IP addresses landed on the home page in a 36-month period, but 56.3 percent of these left the intervention website within 30 seconds (Brouwer et al., e-pub ahead of print). This touches upon the critical issue in Internet-delivered interventions: how can health ever be promoted if people rarely or never use the actual intervention?

Therefore, this chapter will focus on how to stimulate use of Internet-delivered interventions in worksite health promotion. Both the development and the implementation phase will be discussed in this chapter, because the intervention itself *and* the way in which it is implemented contribute to the use of Internet-delivered interventions.

DEVELOPMENT PHASE

User experience refers to what a person thinks and feels during and after a visit to an intervention website. The main idea is that positive user experience leads to increased use. A conceptual framework related to website design in general, as described by Garrett (2002), can also be applied during the development phase to optimize user experience of employees using Internet-delivered interventions aimed at worksite health promotion. Garrett distinguishes five layers (from bottom to top: strategy, scope, structure, skeleton and surface) to conceptualize user experience. The strategy of a website incorporates not only what the intervention wants to establish (i.e. site objectives), but also what the user needs are. This fundamentally determines the scope of these features and functions. The scope is shaped by the structure of a website which defines how the intervention will function (e.g. options involved in performing and completing tasks). The skeleton is a concrete expression of the more abstract structure of a website, and concerns the arrangement of interface elements (e.g. placing important elements, such as navigation menu and search bar, consistently). On the surface, the user perceives the aspects of the design that relate to the visual presentation of interface elements (e.g. typeface, images and navigational components). When making use of an intervention, the employee is first confronted with the surface of an Internet-delivered intervention. However, from the point of view of intervention development, the starting point is the lowest, more abstract layer. Decisions on a lower layer have an influence on the choices available on higher layers. If your site objective is, for example, to let employees monitor their changes in physical activity, then the features and functions at the scope layer should be in line with this site objective. Therefore, during intervention development, work on a higher layer can start, but not finish, before work on a lower layer has finished. All layers should be addressed to optimize user experience, ergo the use of Internet-delivered interventions in worksite health promotion. I will now describe how to apply this framework within the field of worksite health promotion, and will provide examples of the decisions to be made at each level. I will make a distinction between theory-based methods and their practical application and the intervention itself.

Strategy

On the strategy layer, the development team needs to define site objectives and to identify user needs. Research tools like surveys, interviews or focus groups are most suitable for gathering user needs (Garrett, 2002). A good site objective should be formulated "SMART" (Specific, Measurable, Attainable, Realistic and Timely) which would include empirically justifiable statements on what will specifically change (behavior or determinants) and by what period of time. For example, "a 20% increase of employees' knowledge about healthy alternatives to unhealthy food 3 months after release of the website". Knowledge is used here as an example, but Internet-delivered interventions can also be used to teach behavioral skills or to increase motivation regarding behavior change.

Scope and structure: Theory-based methods and their practical application

In gathering requirements for both an intervention's functionality and its content, employees' involvement is highly important (Garrett,

2002). However, during development the format of any content should be in line with its purpose, and the intervention itself should not be a conglomeration of all possible features. A feature should be proven effective, and not be available at an intervention phase for the sake of being available. A recent systematic review showed, for example, that professional support (e.g. ask the expert), although often provided, was used to only a limited extent (Crutzen et al., e-pub ahead of print). Together with user needs, features might be linked to each other and to the site objectives. In my example, the intervention's objective is to increase knowledge. If employees want to increase knowledge in an enjoyable way, the entertainment aspect should be the focus of attention during development. However, if employees want to find information as quickly as possible, this should be the focus of attention during its development. These needs should be translated into functional specifications (including appropriate methods). If employees want to increase knowledge in an enjoyable way, a game (using active learning) could be an appropriate tool. However, if employees want to find information as quickly as possible, a FAQ-webpage (Frequently Asked Questions) seems more appropriate. When gathering requirements for an intervention's functionality and content, these requirements should be in line with the strategy defined on the lower layer. Sometimes it is necessary to revise the strategy if requirements fall outside the scope; certain requirements for an intervention's functionality and content may be lacking or are not recommendable for use online. For example, interventions requiring physiological measurements cannot be completely carried out online. Nevertheless, it is possible that certain interventions require physiological measurements. If that is the case, however, this probably indicates that the development team jumped into gathering requirements too soon (Garrett, 2002) without realizing that the Internet is not the appropriate medium for reaching their health promotion goals. After all, the Internet is only a tool that can be used for worksite health promotion purposes and using the Internet is not a goal on its own.

Skeleton and surface: Intervention

This is probably the moment where health promoters (e.g. HR professionals, occupational health specialists and health and safety specialists) should hand over their activities to people who have more technical and design experience. I recommend involving the technical and design staff in the intervention's development team right from the start to facilitate cooperation with health promoters. The technical and design staff create a prototype, which should be compared with the original health promotion goals (i.e. site objectives). This prototype lays the foundation for the last step: fine-tuning the intervention to lift it to a higher level. Here it is all about detail: a slightly darker background; larger typeface; more narrow buttons; and so on. Toward the end of the development phase, the focus is more and more on the aesthetic sense of user experience.

Checklist for practitioners

1. Identify user needs and define SMART site objectives
2. Involve employees in gathering intervention's requirements
3. Involve technical and design staff in the intervention's development team from the start
4. Introduce implementation policies and practices that foster an implementation climate
5. Make sure that the intervention is perceived as being congruent with employees' values

---

IMPLEMENTATION PHASE

Since implementation of an Internet-delivered intervention is related to the intervention itself, the development phase and implementation phase are interdependent. In other words, decisions made during the development phase have an influence on the implementation of an Internet-delivered intervention. For example, if it is necessary (for functional purposes) to log on to the intervention, then this can have a negative influence on the *perceived* anonymity by the employees. Therefore, it is necessary, in this example, to pay attention to anonymity during the implementation phase.

For Internet-delivered interventions in worksite health promotion, it is an advantage that these interventions are embedded in a social context that could facilitate implementation. Normally, Internet-delivered interventions can be used at one's own convenience. This is usually

178

seen as an advantage but it is also a disadvantage, since people can also leave these interventions "at their own convenience". This has a negative impact from an implementation point of view, since this can lead to interventions not being used properly. Embedding these interventions in a social context can partly counteract this negative impact, because it provides a structure in which the intervention is offered to potential users. To draw a parallel with Internet-delivered interventions that are embedded in a social context by linking them to school activities, the feasibility, appropriateness and effectiveness of such a social context could be explained by the infrastructure being available and intermediaries (e.g. teachers) being accustomed to such settings (e.g. providing education during class hours). In an intervention among high school students, for example, they filled in a monitoring questionnaire in the course of compulsory school activities. Afterwards, on a voluntary basis and during their spare time, students could log on to obtain their individually tailored feedback. More than half of the students (55.7 percent) logged on (Crutzen et al., 2008). So, even though the students were not obliged to visit the website as part of their school requirements, the use of an available infrastructure (e.g. compulsory school activities using computer facilities) during the first time use of the intervention resulted in higher voluntary use outside the social context.

Infrastructures can also be available in worksites, but Internet-delivered interventions are relatively new in worksite health promotion and their implementation is comparable to the implementation of other innovations in worksite settings. Therefore, it is useful to look at the theory on the determinants of effective implementation of innovations in organizations (Figure 16.1).

In line with Weiner et al. (2009), I argue that the theory on the determinants of effective implementation of innovations in organizations

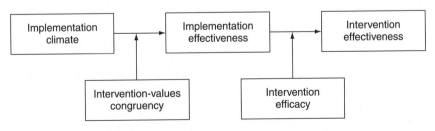

FIGURE 16.1 **Implementation effectiveness and intervention effectiveness**

is applicable to Internet-delivered interventions for the following reasons: (1) adoption of Internet-delivered interventions in worksite health promotion is an authority-based decision process; (2) implementation requires resources (e.g. training); and (3) intervention use by many employees is necessary to produce collective benefits (e.g. productivity and happiness at work). According to this theory, "implementation effectiveness" is a function of the implementation climate that results from the organizational readiness for change, and the quality of the implementation policies and practices. Weiner and colleagues give an example of how to establish such an implementation climate for a smoking cessation intervention. They start with the organizational readiness for change by not only, among other things, organizing an employee advisory board, drafting a new and more restrictive smoking policy that was acceptable to this advisory board and creating a communication plan to inform employees of the new policy, but also by removing ashtrays and installing smoke detectors. It should be noted, however, that organizational readiness for change regarding an intervention aimed at a specific behavior does not automatically apply to interventions aimed at other behaviors as well. Subsequently, the quality of implementation policies and practices was addressed in several ways, which could be considered as separate intervention strategies. For example, not only soliciting employee input on the implementation of the policy, but also adjusting employees' work schedules to participate in the smoking cessation intervention that was going to be offered. Ultimately, this should lead to an implementation climate in which use of the intervention is rewarded, supported and expected. The interaction between implementation climate and the degree to which employees perceive the intervention as being congruent with their values determines the implementation effectiveness as measured by intervention use (Table 16.1). Finally, the interaction between implementation effectiveness (resulting in intervention use) and the efficacy of the intervention determines the true effectiveness of the intervention. In other words, if an intervention is properly implemented but the intervention is not efficacious in promoting worksite health, then the impact of the intervention will be limited. The reverse, however, is also true: if an intervention has the potential to be very efficacious with regard to worksite health promotion but poorly implemented (resulting in the intervention being hardly used), then the impact of the intervention will also be limited. Hence, to assure an impact of Internet-delivered interventions in worksite health

TABLE 16.1 **Intervention use**

Implementation climate	Intervention-values congruency		
	Poor	**Neutral**	**Good**
Strong	Compliant use	Adequate use	Committed, consistent use
Weak	Little or no use	Little or no use	Sporadic, inadequate use

Source: Adapted from Weiner and colleagues (2009).

promotion, these interventions need to be efficacious and properly implemented.

Although the use of Internet-delivered interventions in worksite health promotion is promising, a recent systematic review on participation in worksite health promotion (Robroek et al., 2009) stresses that a multi-component strategy is needed to optimize employees' participation. For example, offer programs with a fitness center or exercise program besides Internet-delivered intervention that mainly focus on education or counselling. The pooled participation levels for multi-component interventions was 43 percent, while this was 28 percent and 26 percent, respectively, for education/counselling and fitness center/exercise programs separately. Furthermore, this systematic review also revealed that there were differences in participation levels between interventions aimed at physical activity and interventions aimed at multiple behaviors: the pooled participation levels for interventions aimed at physical activity was 29 percent while this was 33 percent for interventions aimed at multiple behaviors. This could be explained by employees having a freedom of choice between behaviors that are perceived as being most relevant to them. The advantage of Internet-delivered interventions is that it is easier to offer a broad intervention taking into account different behaviors that are relevant to different employees. In other words, Internet-delivered interventions can be more responsive to user needs. These findings are in line with the idea that interactional richness is the most important predictor of intervention use (from a development point of view). Interactional richness consists of two components: media richness and information richness, because use and satisfaction depend on the medium as well as the information it provides. Media richness is defined as the extent to which a website facilitates user control (e.g. freedom of choice), provides two-way communication and is responsive to user needs. Information richness is defined as visitors' perceptions of the extent to which the website provides relevant, accurate, comprehensible and comprehensive information. Interactional richness has a direct positive relation to utilitarian value (i.e. usefulness) and hedonic value (i.e. appreciation). Together, utilitarian value and hedonic value constitute the two-dimensional concept of user experience. The main idea, as described at the beginning of this chapter, is that positive user experience leads to increased use. So, the responsiveness to user needs, in terms of both the content of the intervention and its functionality, makes the Internet highly appropriate to deliver worksite health promotion interventions. Nevertheless, the Internet should not be seen as the Holy Grail, but as a proper tool to increase the impact of worksite health promotion on employees' well-being.

CHAPTER 17

MITIGATING THE IMPACT OF AN ECONOMIC DOWNTURN ON MENTAL WELL-BEING

Paul Litchfield
BT Group Plc

OVERVIEW

BT has a well-developed mental health framework which seeks to support employees at their different stages of need as well as helping managers deal with mental health issues. The framework has three elements – primary prevention, secondary intervention and tertiary rehabilitation. Products and services have been developed that address the issues of education and training, assessment and practical support for each of these elements. The resultant suite of interventions is known as the company's "mental health toolkit" and is available for deployment by individuals, managers or operational units as required. The toolkit is kept under constant review and is revised and supplemented in the light of both developments in good practice and business requirements.

This approach has served the company well in recent years and the various metrics used to track progress, such as mental-health-related sickness-absence, showed a gradual improvement against a previously rising trend. However, the global financial crisis of 2008 with the consequential economic downturn had a significant impact on the company and its people. The direct effects of the crisis, together with the restructuring made necessary by altered market conditions, hit many BT people hard and this became evident in the various indicators of employee mental well-being. This case study outlines the measures taken to mitigate the impact of these difficult times on the workforce.

BACKGROUND

BT is one of the world's leading providers of communications solutions and services, operating in 170 countries. Its principal activities include the provision of networked IT services; fixed telecommunications services; broadband and Internet products and services; and converged fixed/mobile products and services. BT has four customer-facing business divisions (BT Global Services, Openreach, BT Retail and BT Wholesale) supported by two internal service units (BT Innovate & Design and BT Operate) and a Group Headquarters element – the term applied to each is "Line of Business". The company employs around 101,000 people of whom some 80 percent are located in the United Kingdom. In the year ending 31 March 2010, BT Group had revenues of £20,859 million and pre-tax profits of £1007 million.

An early effect of the financial crisis in the United Kingdom was the collapse of the housing market in 2008. Mortgage funding dried up and house prices tumbled leading to the virtual cessation of new homes being built and a dramatic reduction in all sales. Demand for the provision of telephony and broadband is largely driven by the housing market and therefore this source of work also diminished very substantially leading to, among other things, the disappearance of the requirement for overtime working. Service engineers, many of whom had become used to regular overtime working, therefore experienced a drop in take-home pay just at the time when many household expenses were surging and, in a number of cases, other family members were facing redundancy or entry to an employment market with greatly diminished opportunities. Signs of distress emerged fairly quickly with an increased utilization rate of the employee assistance program and a marked upturn in applications to the BT Benevolent Fund, which deals with cases of employee hardship.

As the recession deepened the impact spread to other parts of the company. As spending by customers fell, competition for market share increased and margins were squeezed. Cost control is the hallmark of a well-run company but the situation demanded significant cost reduction which, in turn, required considerable restructuring. Substantial headcount reductions were achieved without compulsory redundancy but many people were displaced from their roles and redeployed into other activities, often in a different part of the business. The pressures on the people affected, their colleagues and those managing them were considerable.

THE APPROACH

There was a deeply held view, from the most senior levels of the company down, that the organization should do all that it reasonably could to support its people through these difficult times. The mental health framework, together with its components, had proven its worth and the temptation to seek some new "solution" to the problems being encountered was resisted. It was recognized that different parts of the business were facing different pressures against a varying time line and that each had its own "culture", albeit with common elements. The decision was therefore made to develop specific mental health action plans for each of the Lines of Business making use of existing resources from the toolkit as far as possible. Ownership of the plans was vested in each Line of Business leadership team and they were developed in close association with the Group Health Adviser, a clinical psychologist.

The framework is set out in Table 17.1 and the different elements of the toolkit are described below.

TABLE 17.1 **BT mental health framework with "Toolkit" products and services**

	Primary Prevention	Secondary Intervention	Tertiary Rehabilitation
Education & Training	■ Managing Pressure ■ Positive Mentality ■ Management Stress Competencies*	■ STRIDE ■ Mental Health First Aid* ■ Dealing with Distress*	■ Stress Management ■ Open Minds: Head First
Assessment	■ How am I doing?* ■ CARE Agile*	■ STREAM ■ Mental Health Dashboard*	■ Occupational Health Service
Practical support	Achieving the Balance	■ Health & Well-being Passport ■ Employee Assistance Management	■ Guided Self-Help ■ Employee Assistance Program ■ Recession Counseling Service* ■ Cognitive Behavioral Therapy*

Note: * Resources developed or enhanced in response to the economic downturn.

Managing pressure

An online resource designed to help people understand, manage and cope more effectively with stressful situations.

Positive mentality

An online program created with the Sainsbury Center for Mental Health that addresses mental health issues from a personal perspective and promotes improved resilience. The program follows the "ten top ways to look after your mental health" approach from the Mental Health Foundation.[1]

Management stress competencies

The refined framework of management competencies for preventing and reducing stress at work developed by HSE, CIPD and Investors in People[2] was built into a refreshed set of people manager capabilities. The program launched under the title "Becoming a better people manager" seeks to integrate the attributes required to promote good mental health into general standards of management behavior.

How am I doing?

An online self-assessment tool for managers designed to support the revised "Becoming a better people manager" competencies.

CARE Agile

Analysis of data from the company-wide engagement survey showed a quantifiable link between well-being and engagement. The questionnaire, which is sent quarterly to a representative sample of the workforce, was adapted to include views on whether people are being treated fairly and consistently.

Achieving the balance

Practical guidance on flexible working, career/life planning, caring and other responsibilities that may need to be reconciled with work. BT's programs and policies to support attaining a balance suitable for each individual are detailed.

STRIDE

Mandatory online training for people managers to impart knowledge about dealing with stress in members of their team.

Mental health first aid

A one-day workshop based on the program developed in Australia[3] to train line managers and trade union officials in the recognition of mental health problems and how to guide individuals to appropriate professional help.

Dealing with distress

A resource pack outlining the key issues for managers to be aware of when dealing with people in distress. Material includes warning signs to look out for where there is a risk of self-harm and how to access help rapidly in such circumstances.

STREAM

An application built for BT in conjunction with the Trades Unions to identify people with impaired mental health and the work factors which are contributing to their difficulties. The tool creates an individual report recommending control measures that they and their manager can consider and, using anonymized data, generates management reports on organizational stress levels.

Mental health dashboard

A synthesis of data drawn from sickness-absence, Occupational Health Service, Employee Assistance Programme and STREAM reports. The dashboard, which is refreshed monthly, shows trends in the quantity, severity and causation of mental health problems by Line of Business.

Health & well-being passport

A document agreed by people with vulnerabilities, such as recurring mental illness, and their manager supported, if necessary, by specialist disability advisers. It sets out agreed work adjustments and flags both warning signs of deteriorating health and sources of assistance most helpful to the employee.

Employee assistance management

A dedicated team of counselors available to provide telephone advice to managers dealing with difficult situations and to provide close onsite support for the most serious cases.

Stress management

A suite of training materials, delivered either online or in a classroom environment, for employees and managers explaining the nature, causes and management of stress.

Open minds: Head first

A comprehensive and attractively presented downloadable document which explains mental health, how to improve it and the effects that impairment can have on work and daily living. Written by BT people from a very practical perspective, it gives detailed guidance on the approach to dealing with colleagues who are absent with a mental health problem and how best to manage their rehabilitation back into work.

Occupational health service

A network of specialist occupational health nurses and physicians who have been inducted into BT working, policies and procedures. Guidance is given to employees and managers on prognosis and adjustments to facilitate an effective return to work. Complex cases are escalated to a "core" team that provides more intensive support to management.

Guided self-help

Signposting to a range of external publications dealing with psychological issues such as anger management, addiction, depression and compulsions. Resources have been selected for adopting a cognitive behavioral model and a step-by-step self-help approach.

Employee assistance program

A confidential service available free of charge to users 24 hours a day, 7 days a week and 365 days a year. Telephone advice lines cover legal, financial, consumer and benefits issues as well as personal counseling which can progress to face-to-face sessions if required.

Recession counseling services

As part of the UK Government-funded initiative, the charity RELATE set up with BT an online chat service to help employees address the impact of the recession and other financial concerns on relationship issues.

Cognitive behavioral therapy

A case-managed UK-wide service accessed by referral through the company's occupational health service. Users are triaged into a suitable level of service that comprises self-help, coaching or a full CBT program delivered either by telephone or face to face. The aim is to help individuals recover and to support them back to productive employment.

EMBEDDING

Line of Business programs were implemented through their normal management chain using their standard communication channels to reinforce the message that this was part of running an effective business and not some "health initiative" or "bolt on". Progress was monitored by the respective leadership teams and direction was usually vested in the health and safety champion for that part of the company (typically an operational director reporting directly to the Chief Executive of the Line of Business).

Centrally efforts were focussed on raising awareness and securing support at senior level for the measures being taken. Additionally, the toolkit was enhanced by refreshing materials, advancing planned developments and introducing new elements where there was a perceived gap or weakness. Light touch monitoring of business programs was undertaken to ensure that best practice was shared across the company and that any shortcomings were addressed speedily. A particular emphasis was given to addressing the issue of "perceived justice" at a company-wide level (see Box 17.1).

BOX 17.1 **The elements of perceived justice**[4]

There are three key dimensions that influence whether individuals accept that change is being implemented fairly:

- **Distributive justice**. The selection criteria for the individuals and parts of the organization are subject to changes. This incorporates elements related to "needs", such as legislation and collective agreements, as well as "efficiency" which captures skills, productivity, and so on.
- **Procedural justice**. This requires consistent procedures executed without bias and on the basis of accurate information. There must be a trusted mechanism for correcting poor decisions and the system must be founded on ethical and moral standards appropriate for the society in which the organization is operating.
- **Interactional justice**. The nature and timing of internal and external communication are vital in maintaining trust. Clear, early, open and personal communication with those involved is critical in avoiding uncertainty, rumor and de-motivation.

The concepts were embedded in a revised performance management system and the tone of voice in communications relating to people issues was altered to emphasize the company's values, especially in relation to support for colleagues in difficulty.

OUTCOME AND EVALUATION

In an ideal world the recession would have been anticipated and measures would have been put in place in advance to minimize the adverse impact on the company and its people. In practice, the trigger for specific action on mental health was the observed effects on some of the workforce and, even then, it took some time to comprehend the scale and the depth of what was happening. Almost all of the metrics available are lag measures and the elapsed time between an individual's mental ill-health changing and an incident being counted can be many months. Consequently tracking progress is akin to altering course in a large ship – activity in the wheelhouse may be evident on the bridge only after a considerable distance has been traveled.

The adverse trend in dashboard measures continued for many months after action plans were implemented. At a company-wide level there has been a leveling off of all metrics and a decline in those with the shorter lag periods. Those Lines of Business that implemented programs earliest have seen the greatest objective improvement. However, those were also the divisions that encountered difficulties first and it may be that improvement is related more to their position in the economic cycle than any effect of their mental health action plans. As with most activities in the real world, it is possible to note associations between events but almost impossible to prove that there has been any cause and effect. Anecdotal evidence from other companies experiencing similar difficulties suggests that the activity undertaken in BT did limit the scale of the adverse impact on mental health and the duration of the problems.

On a subjective level the outcome is more positive. Feedback on both an individual and a group level indicates that the efforts to promote good mental health and to support people in distress have been well-received. They have reinforced the view that BT is a company that cares about its people and seeks to do the right thing by them, thereby contributing to an improvement in employee engagement.

At a management level, leaders perceive that they have responded appropriately and in a structured fashion to events which are unprecedented in their working lives. Lessons have been learned and the impact on well-being of change management programs is now routinely considered both in the planning of how measures will be implemented and as a criterion of success.

CHAPTER 18

KEEPING PRESSURE POSITIVE: IMPROVING WELL-BEING AND PERFORMANCE IN THE NHS THROUGH INNOVATIVE LEADERSHIP DEVELOPMENT

Jill Flint-Taylor
Robertson Cooper Ltd

Joan Durose
Health Services Management Center,
University of Birmingham

and

Caroline Wigley
NHS West Midlands

OVERVIEW

The subject of this case study is a leadership and well-being theme that was developed as a core component of the National Health Service (NHS) West Midlands Executive Leadership Development (Aspiring Chief Executives) and Aspiring Directors programs. The theme, entitled "Keeping Pressure Positive" (KPP), was designed to challenge participants to raise their game in managing pressure and performance for themselves and others, and to provide developmental support to help them achieve this.

BACKGROUND

Leadership in the National Health Service

As the largest employer in Europe, by 2010 the NHS had approximately 1.3 million staff and an annual budget of just under £110 billion. NHS West Midlands was created in July 2006 as one of ten strategic health authorities (SHAs) tasked with leading the regional NHS and providing a key link between the Department of Health and the local NHS. From the outset, building regional capability and strong leadership in the NHS trusts was identified as an important aspect of the work of the SHAs. NHS trusts are public sector organizations responsible for the delivery of NHS services to the public. During the period described in this case study (2006–2010) there were two main categories of NHS trust – commissioning organizations (providing some services and commissioning others) and provider or commissioned organizations (e.g. hospitals and ambulance services) – with each trust being led by a board consisting of executive and non-executive directors and a non-executive chair. The emergence of this system created a large number of senior leadership roles in each region, and a high demand for strong leadership capability. NHS West Midlands led the way nationally in being the first SHA to deliver a development program for executives at board level in the region's NHS trusts.

The KPP material described here was also introduced in 2009 to the NHS East Midlands Aspiring Chief Executives program and was applied in a range of leadership, well-being and organizational development contexts in other regions. It has also been used widely outside the NHS.

Overall purpose and goals of the programs

The Executive Leadership Development (Aspiring Chief Executives) program was designed in 2006 for Directors on an anticipated trajectory for a Chief Executive role, although the benefit of the program was not intended to depend on participants progressing to a Chief Executive position. The main objective was to identify and develop a strong base of senior leadership talent across the region. The Aspiring Directors program was designed to develop the managerial and leadership capability of middle managers from both commissioning and provider organizations across the West Midlands. Both programs could, therefore, be described more generically as talent management and development programs for senior leaders of high potential. The specific design and objectives of each program reflected the different needs of the two groups. For the purpose of this case study, our detailed discussion focuses mainly on the more senior Executive Leadership program.

Purpose and goals of the "Keeping Pressure Positive" theme

The design of this 10-month program incorporated academic input (e.g. theory of corporate decision-making) with person-centered assessment and development, supported further by coaching, mentoring and action learning sets. Within the person-centered development element, a specific requirement was identified for a theme that would support participants in strengthening their personal and psychological resources and improving their ability to manage their own and others' response to challenging situations and demands.

To meet this requirement, business psychologists Robertson Cooper Ltd worked in collaboration with HSMC at the University of Birmingham and the National School of Government to develop a theme based on Robertson Cooper's "Keeping Pressure Positive" approach towards improving leadership, well-being and organizational performance. The specific objectives of this intervention were to:

- Increase the time, attention and effort spent by participants on improving staff well-being (particularly psychological well-being) and engagement.
- Increase participants' personal resilience (on the assumption that even those with a high level of resilience could benefit from raising it to the next level).
- Develop participants' ability to improve organizational performance by balancing challenge with support for those who report to them, and by addressing other risks to staff well-being within their area of responsibility.

The overall aim of the theme was to improve leadership capability and organizational performance across the region by developing participants' ability to "Keep Pressure Positive" for themselves and others.

THE APPROACH

Design and implementation

A half-day "Keeping Pressure Positive" session was incorporated into each of the program's four residential modules, allowing the opportunity for participants to apply insights, principles and techniques between modules. This is always useful for the transfer and embedding that are essential to effective leadership development. In the case of developing personal resilience and learning to flex your leadership style (two of the main elements of the KPP theme), such opportunities are particularly valuable.

To begin with, the theme was entitled "Personal and Psychological Resources" and was somewhat broader in scope. Early evaluations showed that the core KPP elements were adding the most value, and that it was important to reduce the overlap with other more generic aspects of the personal and psychological side of leadership. This was achieved by focusing the theme more tightly around the core KPP elements, and also by rationalizing the use of psychometric profiling across the different themes and other aspects of the program.

This is an important issue for all leadership development programs. There is no substitute for psychometric profiling in helping participants to engage with the personal style and impact aspects of leadership. It can, however, be tempting to include too many psychometric measures relating to specific topics and approaches. It is important to review the overall impact and value to participants, as surface differences in the psychometric instruments often mask a high level of duplication in the underlying constructs.

In the case of the West Midlands program, an early monitoring exercise led to a review and rationalization of the psychometric measures used across the program. The personality-based *Leadership Impact* profile used in the KPP theme was retained as one of the key psychometric measures.

Following the initial evaluation and adjustments to the program, based on the experience of Cohorts One and Two, the KPP theme settled down into the format that was used for Cohorts Three, Four, Five, Six and Seven (2007–2010).

Keeping pressure positive program

Overview for participants: *The focus of this theme is on keeping pressure positive for yourself and others. As a senior leader in the NHS, it is your responsibility to create a high performance culture characterized by high levels of engagement, well-being and productivity. To achieve this, you need to manage pressure effectively – creating positive pressure by challenging others to raise their game, while balancing this with appropriate levels of support.*

Case study notes: All modules were designed to combine input on key principles, research evidence and practical techniques with interactive learning through discussion, individual reflection, small group work and peer mentoring (in pairs). A "light touch" version of the peer mentoring technique (e.g. Holbeche, 1996) was used in each module, with the emphasis on mutual developmental support by dividing the time strictly into two sections and taking turns to mentor and be mentored. Participants were also provided with guidance on setting up and making use of longer-term peer mentoring relationships with fellow program participants or with other work colleagues.

The program provided both challenges and opportunities in terms of the range of backgrounds, roles and organizational contexts from which participants were drawn. Typical roles including Medical Director, Director of Nursing and Governance, Chief Operating Officer, Director of Finance, Director of Commissioning and Director of Public Health. All participants were from the same region and it was important to set clear expectations around mutual respect and confidentiality. It was important to be aware of inherent structural tensions within the NHS system – in particular between representatives of commissioner and provider organizations – which could have an effect on participants' willingness to share information in an open and transparent way. This was addressed in Module One of each Cohort run (both in the KPP theme and more broadly by theme tutors and others), and experience over all four modules suggested that the program was generally successful in establishing a safe developmental environment for participants.

Module One: Introduction to theme: overview and peer mentoring

Overview for participants: *The first module sets out the business case for "keeping pressure positive", explaining the key concepts of engagement and well-being and outlining their relationship to productivity and organizational performance. This module also introduces the principles and practice of peer mentoring, and sets you*

(Continued)

up to work in peer mentoring pairs to challenge and support each other during, and possibly after, the program.

Case study notes: The two main elements of this module were (a) establishing the business case for the active management of well-being in general and of psychological well-being in particular (e.g. Harter et al., 2003; Robertson and Flint-Taylor, 2010) and (b) introducing participants to peer mentoring. As is often the case with the first module on a topic in an extended program, the challenge here was to provide the necessary background information and input to provide a solid foundation while at the same time actively engaging participants and creating the energy and momentum to get the theme off to a good start. This was achieved by tweaking the interactive exercises based on the experience of running the program with the earlier Cohorts.

Module Two: Keeping pressure positive – a personal perspective: personal coping strategies

Overview for participants: *The second module helps to develop your personal coping strategies. Here we explore your personal resilience profile, which covers the management of frustration, anger, conflict, anxiety and other sources of pressure, as well as the complex issues of self-confidence and self-esteem. We provide a framework and practical tools for taking personal resilience and confidence to the next level – whatever your starting point. These principles and techniques are also useful for coaching those who report to you.*

Case study notes: The design of this module drew on (a) the experience of adapting stress management and resilience development techniques from cognitive behavioral psychology to workplace training and development programs (Proudfoot et al., 1997) and (b) an up-to-date review of research and practice in this area, including the "Resilience Prescription" (Haglund et al., 2007), which summarizes the key practices of those who develop and demonstrate high levels of resilience. The main assumptions that guide the KPP approach to this topic are firstly that resilience is complex and multi-dimensional (most people are more resilient in some ways and in certain situations than in others) and secondly that resilience can be developed.

Evidence from the leadership profiling and experience of working with the West Midlands participants suggested that many were already highly resilient – perhaps unsurprisingly, given the extent of the challenges they typically faced and managed. Nevertheless, this was generally felt to be a highly valuable element of the theme, given the level of challenge in these senior roles.

Module Three: Keeping pressure positive for others: Part I – balancing challenge with support

Overview for participants: *The third module encourages you to explore the impact that your natural leadership style is likely to have on the engagement, motivation and well-being of those who report to you. We look at how you can flex your style and balance challenge with support to enhance the effectiveness of your workgroup or organization.*

Case study notes: Preparation work for this module required participants to complete the *Leadership Impact* questionnaire, a measure of the Five Factor Model of personality that produces an expert report relating the participant's natural style to his or her likely impact on well-being, engagement, morale and motivation in the team (Flint-Taylor, 2008). The session was designed to incorporate input on the *Leadership Impact* framework with individual reflection and peer mentoring. The objective of the session was for each participant to identify two to three aspects of their leadership impact style to work on going forward. This could relate to potential strengths not fully realized yet, or to risks that needed to be managed to avoid having a negative impact on others' well-being. Participants found it particularly useful to consider the idea of "risks in strengths" (similar to de-railers or the "dark side" of personality, but seen from a more positive angle). So, for example, a participant might recognize the risk of being so confident in her own capability that she unintentionally creates a situation where those reporting to her feel de-motivated, disengaged or even stressed by not having their ideas listened to or not being given sufficient responsibility. Participants were encouraged to develop ways of flexing their style to optimize their impact on the well-being, engagement and performance of others.

Module Four: Keeping pressure positive for others: Part II – managing the requirements for engagement and well-being

Overview for participants: *The fourth module provides further support for exploring the actual impact of your leadership style, and goes beyond this to look at how you can manage other aspects of the situation to improve the engagement, well-being and effectiveness of your workgroup and your organization.*

Case study notes: Prior to this module, participants were offered the opportunity to audit levels of psychological well-being and engagement among those who reported to them, using the ASSET questionnaire and reporting system (Faragher et al., 2004). This exercise was entirely voluntary, and participants were encouraged to consider whether it would be useful and appropriate for

---

(Continued)

their group to undertake it as well as make sure they were prepared to communicate and act on the results. The session itself was designed to help participants to discuss and reflect on current levels of well-being and engagement in their area of responsibility, to consider how their own behavior and impact style might relate to this, and to begin to develop a plan for addressing situational factors having a negative impact (e.g. overload, resources or work relationships). As participants were drawn from a wide range of roles and organizational contexts, this session provided a particularly good forum for the exchange of ideas on issues and possible solutions at a strategic level across the region.

OUTCOMES AND EVALUATION

Both the Executive Leadership (Aspiring Chief Executives) and Aspiring Directors programs were ongoing at the time of writing, so the final evaluation was not available. However, evaluation by the leading organizations (HSMC at the University of Birmingham and NHS West Midlands) has been ongoing. From this it was reported that participants had particularly benefitted from three aspects of the program:

(i)   Providing a theoretical framework within which they can examine both the context of their roles in the NHS and also the personal styles which they most frequently employ.
(ii) Using online tools to reflect their preferred leadership style and the current perceptions of their teams.
(iii) Working with fellow participants in peer mentoring relationships to explore the implications of their styles and the possible changes they might make.

In post-program follow-up interviews by an independent third party, the KPP theme, together with the "Leadership as Performance" elements of the Aspiring Chief Executive program, were the components which generated most frequent and most positive responses from participants when asked the open question: "Which aspects of the programme did you find most useful or interesting?"

A number of interviewees made specific mention of the very immediate way they had been able to apply their learning from the KPP theme in their own day-to-day professional leadership roles. For a number of the clinicians participating in the program, this theme was particularly highlighted as one that gave them the opportunity not just for reflection but also for understanding and articulating their own role as leader and the impact of their behavior on other team members.

Particular applications mentioned included:

- Ability to cope with "failure" in not securing a new role and learning positively from the feedback.
- Understanding of different approaches to handling pressure within own team.
- Newfound confidence to "surface" issues of stress and pressure within team and with peers.
- Openness to considering new career routes/paths.
- Thinking about pressure and resilience in relation to whole life events rather than simply those at work.

The summary evaluation report from the first two Cohorts of the Aspiring Director program notes that they had found useful the "Keeping Pressure Positive Theme and especially the *Leadership Impact* questionnaire. Working with their peer mentors, participants said they found the opportunity to discuss in detail their report feedback extremely valuable and had been able to use the data to inform their developing leadership skills" (Evaluation Report April 2010). Specific observations related to the accuracy and usefulness of the *Leadership Impact* report, and to the practicality, relevance and usefulness of the theme as a whole. Similar observations were made by participants in the East Midlands Aspiring Chief Executive program.

These were the positive messages that led to the KPP theme being seen as a valuable core part of the programs. There were, however, many learning points and issues to iron out along the way. Some of these have been mentioned above. Others relate to the difficulty of accommodating different perspectives, needs and learning styles, and of ensuring that busy leaders engage with the embedding and transfer activities, both between modules and after the program. While much was done on these programs to facilitate immediate and ongoing engagement with the material, this remains one of the key challenges for such interventions. Group size was an important factor here – it became clear that any more than 25 would lose the personal impact, while fewer than 15 would not enable sufficient shared learning.

A full evaluation of the KPP element of these programs would provide a more formal assessment of personal development outcomes for participants. It would also need to include outcome measures related to the leaders' impact on employee well-being and organizational performance. While it would not be possible to draw conclusions about direct, causal relationships between the KPP theme and these outcome measures, it is always important to collect and review this type of information to monitor and explore the impact of such developmental interventions.

NOTES

10   IMPROVING EMPLOYEE ENGAGEMENT AND WELL-BEING IN AN NHS TRUST

1. See http://www.nhshealthandwellbeing.org/ (November 2010).

12   ENGAGING IN HEALTH AND WELL-BEING

1. For more information about the case-studies, or about vielife, please visit www.vielife.com.
2. Food, Nutrition, Physical Activity and the Prevention of Cancer, A Global Perspective. World Cancer Research Fund. 2007 http://www.wcrf-uk.org/research/cp_report.php (July 2010).
3. British Heart Foundation: http://www.bhf.org.uk/keeping_your_heart_healthy/Default.aspx (July 2010).
4. Diabetes UK: http://www.diabetes.org.uk/Guide-to-diabetes/Healthy_lifestyle (July 2010).

17   MITIGATING THE IMPACT OF AN ECONOMIC DOWNTURN ON MENTAL WELL-BEING

1. How to look after your mental health. Mental Health Foundation (London: 2008) http://www.mentalhealth.org.uk/campaigns/look-after-your-mental-health/?locale=en (July 2010).
2. Line management behavior and stress at work: Refined framework for line managers. Chartered Institute of Personnel & Development (London: 2009) http://www.cipd.co.uk/NR/rdonlyres/A6680134-C1CF-4BD6-9B03-311AE 62E8DAF/0/stress_at_work_framework_line_managers.pdf (July 2010).
3. Mental Health First Aid. http://www.mhfa.com.au/documents/Summary_%20MHFA_31_May_09.pdf (July 2010).
4. Kieselbach, T. (ed.) (2009). *Health in Restructuring: Innovative Approaches and Policy Recommendations*. Bremen: University of Bremen http://www.ipg.uni-bremen.de/research/hires/HIRES_FR_090518_english.pdf (July 2010).

REFERENCES

Abramson, L.Y., Seligman, M.E.P. and Teasdale, J.D. (1978) Learned helplessness in humans – critique and reformulation. *Journal of Abnormal Psychology, 87*, 49–74.

Alimo-Metcalfe, B., Alban-Metcalfe, J., Bradley, M., Mariathasan, J. and Samele, C. (2008) The impact of engaging leadership on performance, attitudes to work and wellbeing at work: A longitudinal study. *Journal of Health Organization and Management, 22*, 586–598.

Amabile, T.M., Barsade, S.G., Mueller, J.S. and Staw, B.M. (2005) Affect and creativity at work. *Administrative Science Quarterly, 50*, 367–403.

Arnst, C. (2009) 10 Ways to Cut Health-Care Costs Right Now. *Bloomberg Businessweek*, November 23 (also November 12, 2009) http://www.businessweek.com/magazine/content/09_47/b4156034717852.htm.

Arvey, R.D., Carter, G.W. and Buerkley, D.K. (1991) Job satisfaction. In C.L. Cooper and I.T. Robertson (eds), *International Review of Industrial and Organizational Psychology*. Chichester, UK: John Wiley and Sons Ltd.

Attridge, M. (2009) Measuring and managing employee work engagement: A review of the research and business literature. *Journal of Workplace Behavioral Health, 24*, 383–398.

Avey, J.B., Luthans, F., Smith, R.M. and Palmer, N.F. (2010) Impact of positive psychological capital on employee well-being over time. *Journal of Occupational Health Psychology, 15*, 17–28.

Beck, T., Ward, C.H., Mendelson, M., Hock, J. and Erbaugh, J. (1961) An inventory for measuring depression. *Archives of General Psychiatry, 7*, 158–216.

Berkman, P.L. (1971) Measurement of mental health in a general population survey. *American Journal of Epidemiology, 94*, 105–111.

Black, C. (2008) *Working for a Healthier Tomorrow – Dame Carol Black's Review of the Health of Britain's Working Age Population*. London: Department of Health.

Bond, F.W. and Bunce, D. (2000) Mediators of change in emotion-focused and problem-focused worksite stress management interventions. *Journal of Occupational Health Psychology, 5*, 156–163.

Bond, F.W. and Bunce, D. (2003) The role of acceptance and job control in mental health, job satisfaction, and work performance. *Journal of Applied Psychology, 88*, 1057–1067.

Boorman, S. (2009) *NHS Health and Well-being – Final Report*. London: Department of Health.

Bouchard, T.J. and Loehlin, J.C. (2001) Genes, evolution, and personality. *Behavior Genetics, 31,* 243–273.

Boyce, R.W., Boone, E.L., Cioci, B.W. and Lee, A.H. (2008) Physical activity, weight gain and occupational health among call centre employees. *Occupational Medicine, 58,* 238–244.

Brickman, P., Coates, D. and Janoff-Bulman, R. (1978) Lottery winners and accident victims: Is happiness relative? *Journal of Personality and Social Psychology, 36,* 917–927.

Brouwer, W., Oenema, A., Raat, H., Crutzen, R., De Nooijer, J., De Vries, N.K. and Brug, J. (2010) Characteristics of visitors and revisitors of an Internet-delivered computer-tailored lifestyle intervention implemented for use by the general public. *Health Education Research, 25,* 585–595.

Burch, G.J. St. and Anderson, N. (2008) Personality as a predictor of work-related behaviour and performance: Recent advances and directions for future research. In G. Hodgkinson and J.K. Ford (eds), *International Review of Industrial and Organizational Psychology, Volume 28.* Chichester, UK: John Wiley and Sons Ltd.

Burns, M.O. and Seligman, M.E.P. (1989) Explanatory style across the lifespan: Evidence for stability over 52 years. *Journal of Personality and Social Psychology, 56,* 471–477.

Byron, K. (2005) A meta-analytic review of work – family conflict and its antecedents. *Journal of Vocational Behavior, 67,* 169–198.

Chida, Y. and Steptoe, A. (2008) Positive psychological well-being and mortality: A quantitative review of prospective observational studies. *Psychosomatic Medicine, 70,* 741–756.

Cohn, M. and Fredrickson, B. (2009) Positive emotions. In S.J. Lopez and C.R. Snyder *Oxford Handbook of Positive Psychology.* Oxford: Oxford University Press.

Colquitt, J.A., Greenberg, J. and Zapata-Phelan, C.P. (2005) What is organizational justice? A historical overview. In J. Greenberg and J.A. Colquitt (eds), *Handbook of Organizational Justice.* Mahwah, NJ: Erlbaum.

Cropanzano, R. and Wright, T.A. (1999) A 5-year study of change in the relationship between well-being and performance. *Consulting Psychology Journal: Practice and Research, 51,* 252–265.

Crutzen, R., De Nooijer, J., Brouwer, W., Oenema, A., Brug, J. and De Vries, N.K. (In press) Strategies to facilitate exposure to internet-delivered health behaviour change interventions aimed at adolescents or young adults: A systematic review. *Health Education & Behavior, 38.*

Crutzen, R., De Nooijer, J., Candel, M.J.J.M. and De Vries, N.K. (2008) Adolescents who intend to change multiple health behaviours choose greater exposure to an internet-delivered intervention. *Journal of Health Psychology, 13*(7), 906–911.

Csikszentmihalyi, M. (1990) *Flow: The Psychology of Optimal Experience.* New York: Harper.

DeNeve, K.M. and Cooper, H. (1998) The happy personality: A meta-analysis of 137 personality traits and subjective well-being. *Psychological Bulletin, 124,* 197–229.

Department of Health (DoH) (2004) *Choosing Health: Making Healthy Choices Easier, November*. London: Department of Health.

Department for Work and Pensions and Department of Health (DWP and DoH) (2008) Improving health and work: Changing lives: The Government's Response to Dame Carol Black's Review of the health of Britain's working-age population, accessed by Internet at http://www.workingforhealth.gov.uk/Government-response/ (November 2008).

Diener, E. (2000) Subjective well-being: The science of happiness and a proposal for a national index. *American Psychologist, 55*, 34–43.

Diener, E., Emmons, R.A., Larsen, R.J. and Griffin, S. (1985) The satisfaction with life scale. *Journal of Personality Assessment, 49*, 71–75.

Dienstbier, R.A. (1989) Arousal and physiological toughness: Implications for mental and physical health. *Psychological Review, 96*, 84–100.

Donald, I., Taylor, P., Johnson, S., Cooper, C., Cartwright, S. and Robertson, S. (2005) Work environments, stress and productivity: An examination using ASSET. *International Journal of Stress Management, 12*, 409–423.

Dooris, M. (2001) The health promoting university: A critical exploration of theory and practice. *Health Education, 101*, 51–60.

Dooris, M. (2005) Healthy settings: Challenges to generating evidence of effectiveness. *Health Promotion International, 21*, 55–65.

Dooris, M. and Doherty, S. (2010) Healthy universities – time for action: A qualitative research study exploring the potential for a national programme. *Health Promotion International, 25*, 94–106.

Dorman, C. and Kaiser, D. (2002) Job conditions and customer satisfaction. *European Journal of Work and Organizational Psychology, 11*, 257–283.

Faragher, E.B., Cooper, C.L. and Cartwright, S. (2004) A shortened stress evaluation tool (ASSET). *Stress and Health, 20*, 189–201.

Flade, P. (2003) Britain's workforce lacks inspiration. *Gallup Management Journal*, 11 December 2003.

Flint-Taylor, J. (2008) Too much of a good thing? Leadership strengths as risks to well-being and performance in the team, The British Psychological Society Division of Occupational Psychology Annual Conference, Stratford, January 2007.

Flint-Taylor, J. and Robertson, I.T. (2007) Leaders' Impact on Well-Being and Performance: An Empirical Test of a Model, paper presented at the British Psychological Society, Division of Occupational Psychology, Annual Conference, Bristol, January 2007.

Foresight Mental Capital and Wellbeing Project (2008) *Final Project Report*. London: The Government Office for Science.

Fox, K.R. (1999) The influence of physical activity on mental well-being. *Public Health Nutrition, 2*, 411–418.

Fredrickson, B.L. (1998) What good are positive emotions? *Review of General Psychology, 2*, 300–319.

Fredrickson, B.L. and Joiner, T. (2002) Positive emotions trigger upward spirals towards emotional well-being. *Psychological Science, 13*, 172–175.

Fredrickson, B.L. and Losada, M.F. (2005) Positive affect and the complex dynamics of human flourishing. *American Psychologist, 60*, 678–686.

Fredrickson, B.L., Mancuso, R.A., Branigan, C. and Tugade, M.M. (2000) The undoing effect of positive emotions. *Motivation and Emotion, 24,* 237–258.

Fujita, F. and Diener, E. (2005) Life satisfaction set point: Stability and change. *Journal of Personality and Social Psychology, 88,* 158–164.

Garrett, J.J. (2002) *The Elements of User Experience: User-centered Design for the Web.* Berkeley, CA: New Riders Press.

Gilbreath, B. (2004) Creating healthy workplaces. The supervisor's role. In C.L. Cooper and I.T. Robertson (eds), *International Review of Industrial and Organizational Psychology* (Vol. 18, pp. 93–118). Chichester, UK: Wiley.

Gilbreath, B. and Benson, P.G. (2004) The contribution of supervisor behaviour to employee psychological well-being. *Work & Stress, 18,* 255–266.

Gillespie, B.M., Chaboyer, W., Wallis, M. and Grimbeek, P. (2007) Resilience in the operating room: Developing and testing of a resilience model. *Journal of Advanced Nursing, 59,* 427–438.

Grandey, A. (2000) Emotion regulation in the workplace: A new way to conceptualize emotional labor. *Journal of Occupational Health Psychology, 5,* 95–110.

Great Place to Work (2004) *Europe's Hundred Best Workplaces.* Copenhagen Denmark: Great Place to Work.

Griffeth, R.W., Hom, P.W. and Gaertner, S. (2000) A meta-analysis of antecedents and correlates of employee turnover: Update, moderator tests, and research implications for the next millennium. *Journal of Management, 26,* 463–488.

Haglund, M.E.M., Nestadt, P.S., Cooper, N.S., Southwick, S.M. and Charney, D.S. (2007) Psychobiological mechanisms of resilience: Relevance to prevention and treatment of stress-related psychopathology. *Development and Psychopathology, 19,* 889–920.

Harter, J.K., Schmidt, F.L. and Hayes, T.L. (2002) Business unit level outcomes between employee satisfaction, employee engagement and business outcomes: A meta-analysis. *Journal of Applied Psychology, 87,* 268–279.

Harter, J.K., Schmidt, F.L. and Keyes, C.L.M. (2003) Well-being in the workplace and its relationship to business outcomes: A review of the Gallup studies. In C.L.M. Keyes and J. Haidt (eds), *Flourishing, Positive Psychology and the Life Well-lived.* Washington D.C., USA: American Psychological Society.

Harter, J.K., Schmidt, F.L., Kilham, E.A. and Agrawal, S. (2009) *Q12 Meta-analysis: The Relationship between Engagement at Work and Organizational Outcomes.* USA: Gallup Inc.

Hassmen, P., Koivula, N. and Uutela, A. (2000) Physical exercise and psychological wellbeing: A population study in Finland. *Preventative Medicine, 30,* 17–25.

Hayes, D. and Ross, C.E. (1986) Body and mind: The effect of exercise, overweight and physical health on psychological well-being. *Journal of Health and Social Behaviour, 27,* 387–400.

Hayes, S.C., Bond, F.W., Barnes-Holmes, D. and Austin, J. (eds) (2006) *Acceptance and Mindfulness at Work.* New York: The Haworth Press. Co-published simultaneously as: *Journal of Organizational Behavior Management,* *26*(1/2).

Headey, B. and Wearing, A. (1989) Personality, life events, and subjective well-being: Toward a dynamic equilibrium model. *Journal of Personality and Social Psychology, 57,* 731–739.

Hewitt (2004) Employee engagement higher at double digit companies. Hewitt Associates LLC, Research Brief www.hewitt.com/doubledigitgrowth (July 2010).

Hills, P. and Argyle, M. (2002) The Oxford Happiness Questionnaire: A compact scale for the measurement of psychological well-being. *Personality and Individual Differences, 33,* 1073–1082.

Hodges, T.D. and Asplund, J. (2010) Strengths development in the workplace. In P.A. Linley, S. Harrington and N. Garcea (eds), *Oxford Handbook of Positive Psychology and Work.* Oxford: Oxford University Press.

Holbeche, L. (1996) Peer mentoring: The challenges and opportunities. *Career Development International, 1,* 24–27.

Holdsworth, L. and Cartwright, S. (2003) Empowerment, stress and satisfaction: An exploratory study of a call centre. *Leadership and Organization Development Journal, 24,* 131–140.

Hooker, H., Neathey, F., Casebourne, J. and Munro, M. (2006) *The Third Work Life Balance Employees' Survey. Employment Relations Research Series Number 58,* Brighton, UK: Institute for Employment Studies.

Isaac, F. and Flynn, P. (2001) Johnson & Johnson LIVE FOR LIFE program: Now and then. *American Journal of Health Promotion, 15,* 366. "Health and Wellness at Johnson & Johnson – Jessie's Story," originally on Johnson & Johnson Health Channel, available to public on http://www.youtube.com/watch?v=dTWdnfGcI9s (July 2010).

Isen, A.M. (2009) A role for neuropsychology in understanding the facilitating influence of positive affect on social behaviour. In S.J. Lopez and C.R. Snyder (eds), *Oxford Handbook of Positive Psychology.* Oxford: Oxford University Press.

Johnson & Johnson (2009) Johnson & Johnson Annual Report.

Johnson, S. and Cooper, C. (2003) The construct validity of the ASSET stress measure. *Stress and Health, 19,* 181–185.

Jones, G., Hanton, S. and Connaughton, D. (2002) What is this thing called mental toughness? An investigation of elite sports performers. *Journal of Applied Sport Psychology, 14,* 205–218.

Kaplan, R. (2006) Lopsidedness in leaders: Strategies for assessing it and correcting it. In R.J. Burke and C.L. Cooper (eds), *Inspiring Leaders.* Abingdon, UK: Routledge.

Kaplan, R.S. and Norton, D.P. (1996) *The Balanced Scorecard: Translating Strategy into Action.* Boston, MA: Harvard Business Press.

Khobasha, D.M. and Maddi, S.R. (1999) Early experiences in hardiness development. *Consulting Psychology: Practice and Research, 51,* 106–116.

Kirkaldy, B.D., Levine, R. and Shephard, R.J. (2000) The impact of working hours on physical and psychological health of German managers. *European Review of Applied Psychology, 50,* 443–449.

Kuper, H. and Marmot, M. (2003) Job strain, job demands, decision latitude, and risk of coronary heart disease within the Whitehall II study. *Journal of Epidemiology and Community Health, 57*, 147–153.

Landeweerd, J.A. and Boumans, N.P.G. (1994) The effect of work dimensions and need for autonomy on nurses' work satisfaction and health. *Journal of Occupational and Organizational Psychology, 67*, 207–217.

Leiter, M.P., Harvie, P. and Frizell, C. (1998) The correspondence of patient satisfaction and nurse burnout. *Social Science and Medicine, 47*, 1611–1617.

Lewig, K. and Dollard, M. (2003) Emotional dissonance, emotional exhaustion and job satisfaction in call centre workers. *European Journal of Work and Organizational Psychology, 2*, 366–392.

Lewis, S. (2003) Flexible working arrangements: Implementation, outcomes and management. In C.L. Cooper and I.T. Robertson (eds), *International Review of Industrial and Organizational Psychology*. Chichester, UK: John Wiley and Sons Ltd.

Locke, E.A. (1976) The nature and causes of job satisfaction. In M.D. Dunnette (ed.), *Handbook of Industrial and Organizational Psychology*. Chicago: Rand McNally.

Locke, E.A. and Latham, G.P. (2002) Building a practically useful theory of goal-setting and task motivation: A 35 year odyssey. *American Psychologist, 57*, 705–717.

Locke, E.A. and Latham, G.P. (2009) Science and ethics: What should count as evidence against the use of goal setting? *Academy of Management Perspectives, 34*, 88–91.

Lucas, R.E., Clark, A.E., Georgellis, Y. and Diener, E. (2004) Unemployment alters the set point for life satisfaction. *Psychological Science, 15*, 8–13.

Lundin, A. and Tomas, H. (2009) Unemployment and suicide. *The Lancet, 374*, 270–271.

Luoma, J.B., Hayes, S.C. and Walser, R.D. (2007) *Learning ACT: An Acceptance and Commitment Training Manual for Therapists*. Oakland California: New Harbinger Publications Inc.

Lyubomirsky, S., King, L. and Diener, E. (2005) The benefits of frequent positive affect: Does happiness lead to success? *Psychological Bulletin, 131*, 803–855.

Macey, W.H. and Schneider, B. (2008) The meaning of employee engagement. *Industrial and Organizational Psychology: Perspectives on Science and Practice, 1*, 3–30.

Macleod, D. and Clarke, N. (2009) Engaging for Success: Enhancing employee performance through employee engagement. A report to Government. London, UK: Department for Business Innovation and Skills.

Maddi, S.R. and Khobasha, D.M. (2005) *Resilience at Work*. New York: AMACOM.

Mann, S. (1999) Emotion at work: To what extent are we expressing, suppressing, or faking it? *European Journal of Work and Organizational Psychology, 8*, 347–369.

Martin, U. and Schinke, S.P. (1998) Organizational and individual factors influencing job satisfaction and burnout of mental health workers. *Social Work in Health Care, 28*(2), 51–62.

Martin-Krumm, C.P., Sarrizin, P.G., Peterson, C. and Famose, J.-P. (2003) Explanatory style and resilience after sports failure. *Personality and Individual Differences, 35*, 1685–1695.

McKee-Ryan, F.M., Song, Z., Wanberg, C.R. and Kinicki, A. (2005) Psychological and physical well-being during unemployment: A meta-analytic study. *Journal of Applied Psychology, 90*, 53–76.

Meijman, T.F., Mulder, G., Van Dormolen, M. and Cremer, R. (1992) Workload of driving examiners: A psychophysiological field study. In H. Kragt (ed.), *Enhancing Industrial Performances* (pp. 245–260). London: Taylor & Francis.

Mesmer-Magnus, J.R. and Viswesvaran, C. (2006) How family-friendly work environments affect work/family conflict: A meta-analytic examination. *Journal of Labor Research, 4*, 555–574.

Mezulis, A.H., Abramson, L.Y. and Hankin, B.J. (2004) Is there a universal positivity bias in attributions? A meta-analytic review of individual, developmental, and cultural differences in the self-serving attributional bias. *Psychological Bulletin, 130*, 711–747.

Moliner, C., Martinez-Tur, V., Ramos, J., Peiro, J.M. and Cropanzano, R. (2008) Organizational justice and extra-role customer service: The mediating role of well-being at work. *European Journal of Work and Organizational Psychology, 17*, 327–348.

Morrill, C., Buller, D., Buller, M. and Larkey, L. (1999) Towards an organizational perspective on identifying and managing formal gatekeepers. *Qualitative Sociology, 22*, 51–72.

Morris, J.A. and Feldman, D.C. (1996) The dimensions, antecedents, and consequences of emotional labor. *Academy of Management Review, 21*, 986–1010.

Myers, D.G. (2000) The funds, friends and faith of happy people. *American Psychologist, 55*, 56–67.

National Institute for Health and Clinical Excellence (NICE) (2009) *Methods for Development of NICE Public Health Guidance,* accessed by Internet at: http://www.nice.org.uk/aboutnice/howwework/developingnicepublic healthguidance/publichealthguidanceprocessandmethodguides/public_ health_guidance_process_and_method_guides.jsp?domedia=1&mid= F6A97CF4-19B9-E0B5-D42B4018AE84DD51 (November 2009).

Nelson, D., Basu, R. and Purdie, R. (1998) An examination of exchange quality and work stressors in leader–follower dyads. *International Journal of Stress Management, 5*, 103–112.

Ordonez, L., Schweitzer, M.E., Galinsky, A.D. and Bazerman, M.H. (2009) Goals gone wild: How goals systematically harm individuals and organizations. *Academy of Management Perspectives, 23*, 6–16.

Ozminkowski, R., Ling, D., Goetzel, R.Z., Bruno, J.A., Rutter, K.R., Isaac, F. and Wang, S. (2002) Long-term impact of Johnson & Johnson's health & wellness program on health care utilization and expenditures. *Journal of Occupational & Environmental Medicine, 44*, 21–29.

Parker, H. (2010) *Evaluation report for NHS West Midlands SHA.* Birmingham: Health Services Management Centre, University of Birmingham.

Paton, K., Sengupta, S. and Hassan, L. (2005) Settings, systems and organization development: The healthy living and working model. *Health Promotion International, 20,* 81–89.

Patterson, M., Warr, P. and West, M. (2004) Organizational climate and company productivity: The role of employee affect and employee level. *Journal of Occupational and Organizational Psychology, 77,* 193–216.

Penedo, F.J. and Dahn, J.R. (2005) Exercise and well-being: A review of mental and physical health benefits associated with physical activity. *Current Opinion in Psychiatry. Behavioural Medicine, 18,* 189–193.

Perkins, R., Farmer, P. and Litchfield, P. (2009) *Realising Ambitions: Better Employment Support for People with a Mental Health Condition.* London: The Stationery Office.

Podsakoff, N.P., LePine, J.P. and LePine, M.A. (2007) Differential challenge stressor–hindrance stressor relationships with job attitudes, turnover intentions, turnover, and withdrawal behavior: A meta-analysis. *Journal of Applied Psychology, 92,* 438–454.

Proudfoot, J., Guest, D., Carson, J., Dunn, G., Finlay, H. and Gray, J. (1997) Managing resilience: An occupational attributional training programme. *The Lancet, 350*(9071), 96–100.

Proudfoot, J.G., Coor, P.J., Guest, D.E. and Dunn, G. (2008) Cognitive-behavioural training to change attributional style improves employee well-being, job satisfaction, productivity, and turnover. *Personality and Individual Differences, 46,* 147–153.

Robertson, I.T. and Cooper, C.L. (2009) Full engagement: the integration of employee engagement and psychological well-being. *Leadership & Organization Development Journal, 31,* 324–336.

Robertson, I.T. and Flint-Taylor, J. (2009) Leadership, psychological well-being and organizational outcomes. In S. Cartwright and C.L. Cooper (eds), *Oxford Handbook on Organizational Well-Being.* Oxford: Oxford University Press.

Robertson, I.T. and Flint-Taylor, J. (2010) Well-being in healthcare organizations: Key issues *British Journal of Healthcare Management, 16,* 18–23.

Robertson, I.T. and Smith, M. (1985) *Motivation and Job Design: Theory, Research and Practice.* London: IPM.

Robinson, D., Perryman, S. and Hayday, S. (2004) *The Drivers of Employee Engagement.* Brighton, UK: Institute for Employment Studies.

Robroek, S.J.W., Van Lenthe, F.J., Van Empelen, P. and Burdorf, A. (2009) Determinants of participation in worksite health promotion programmes: A systematic review. *International Journal of Behavioral Nutrition and Physical Activity, 6,* 26.

Rowh, M. (2010) Spousal Support. *Human Resource Executive,* online http://www.hreonline.com/HRE/story.jsp?storyId=456550346 (January 2011).

Russell Investment Group (2007) *Evaluation of Fortune "100 Best Companies to Work For".* Tacoma, WA, USA: Russell Investment Group.

Ryff, C.D. and Keyes, C.L.M. (1995) The structure of psychological well-being revisited. *Journal of Personality and Social Psychology, 69,* 719–727.

Ryff, C.D., Singer, B.H. and Love, G.D. (2004) Positive health: Connecting well-being with biology. *Philosophical Transactions of the Royal Society, 359*, 1383–1394.

Sainsbury Centre for Mental Health (Undated) *Mental Health at Work: Developing the Business case. Policy Paper 8*. London: Sainsbury Centre for Mental Health.

Schaufeli, W.B., Salanova, M., Gonzalez-Romá, V. and Bakker, A.B. (2002) The measurement of engagement and burnout: A confirmative analytic approach. *Journal of Happiness Studies, 3*, 71–92.

Seligman, M.E.P. and Csikszentmihalyi, M. (2000) Positive psychology: An introduction. *American Psychologist, 55*, 5–14.

Snelgrove, S.R. and Phil, H.M. (2001) Occupational stress and job satisfaction: A comparative study of health visitors, district nurses and community psychiatric nurses. *Journal of Nursing Management, 6*, 97–104.

Sonnentag, S. and Zjistra, F.R.H. (2006) Job characteristics and off-job activities as predictors of need for recovery, well-being, and fatigue. *Journal of Applied Psychology, 91*, 330–350.

Sosik, J.J. and Godshalk, V.M. (2000) Leadership styles, mentoring functions received, and job-related stress: A conceptual model and preliminary study. *Journal of Organizational Behavior, 21*, 365–390.

Sparks, K., Cooper, C., Fried, Y. and Shirom, A. (1997) The effects of hours of work on health: A meta-analytic review. *Journal of Occupational and Organizational Psychology, 70*, 391–409.

Springer, K.W and Hauser, R.M. (2006) An assessment of the construct validity of Ryff's scales of psychological well-being: Method, mode, and measurement effects. *Social Science Research, 35*, 1080–1102.

Stairs, M., Galpin, M., Page, N. and Linley, A. (2006) Retention on a knife edge: The role of employee engagement in talent management. *Selection and Development Review, 22*, 19–23.

Steel, P. and Ones, D. (2002) Personality and happiness: A national level analysis. *Journal of Personality and Social Psychology, 83*, 767–781.

Towers Perrin (2003) Working Today. Understanding what drives employee engagement. Towers Perrin Talent Report.

Towers Perrin (2007) Global workforce study. Available from www.towers watson.com.

Towers Perrin (2008a) Webex Engaging employees through effective rewards communication, http://www.towersperrin.com/tp/getwebcachedoc?webc= USA/2008/200809/Towers_Perrin_Total_Rewards_Webcast_Presentation_ FINAL.pdf (July 2010).

Towers Perrin (2008b) Confronting myths: What really matters in attracting, engaging and retaining your workforce. UK: Towers Perrin.

Tugade, M.M. and Fredrickson, B.L. (2004) Resilient individuals use positive emotions to bounce back from negative emotional experiences. *Journal of Personality and Social Psychology, 86*, 320–333.

Van der Hulst, M. (2003) Long work hours and health. *Scandinavian Journal of Work, Environment and Health, 2*, 171–188.

Van Dierendonck, D., Haynes, C., Borrill, C. and Stride, C. (2004) Leadership behavior and subordinate well-being. *Journal of Occupational Health Psychology, 9*(2), 165–175.

Waddell, G. and Burton, A.K. (2006) *Is Work Good for Your Health and Well-Being?* London: The Stationery Office.

Waterman, A.S. (2007) On the importance of distinguishing hedonia and eudaimonia when contemplating the hedonic staircase. *American Psychologist, September*, 612–613.

Watson, D., Clark, L.A. and Tellegen, A. (1988) Development and validation of a brief measure of positive and negative affect: The PANAS Scales. *Journal of Personality and Social Psychology, 54*, 1063–1070.

Weiner, B.J., Lewis, M.A. and Linnan, L.A. (2009) Using organization theory to understand the determinants of effective implementation of worksite health promotion programs. *Health Education Research, 24*, 292–305.

Weiss, A., Bates, T.C. and Luciano, M. (2008) Happiness is a personal(ity)thing: The genetics of personality and well-being in a representative sample. *Psychological Science, 19*, 205–210.

Winwood, P.C., Bakker, A.B. and Winefield, A.H. (2007) An investigation of the role of non–work-time behavior in buffering the effects of work strain. *Journal of Occupational and Environmental Medicine, 49*, 862–871.

World Health Organization (WHO) (1986) *The Ottawa Charter for Health Promotion*, accessed by Internet at http://www.euro.who.int/en/who-we-are/policy-documents/ottawa-charter-for-health-promotion (July 2010).

Wright, T.A. and Bonett, D.G. (1992) The effect of turnover on work satisfaction and mental health: Support for a situational perspective. *Journal of Organizational Behaviour, 13*, 603–615.

Wright, T.A. and Bonett, D.G. (2007) Job satisfaction and psychological well-being as non-additive predictors of workplace turnover. *Journal of Management, 33*, 141–160.

Wright, T.A. and Cropanzano, R. (1997) Well-being, satisfaction and job performance: Another look at the happy/productive worker hypothesis. In L.N. Dosier and J.B. Keys. (eds), *Academy of Management Best Paper Proceedings*, pp. 334–368. Academy of Management.

Wright, T.A. and Cropanzano, R. (2000) Psychological well-being and job satisfaction as predictors of job performance. *Journal of Occupational Health Psychology, 5*, 84–94.

Yarker, J., Donaldson-Feilder, E., Lewis, R. and Flaxman, P.E. (2008) *Management Competencies for Preventing and Reducing Stress at Work: Identifying and Developing the Management Behaviours Necessary to Implement the HSE Management Standard: Phase 2*. London: HSE Books.

AUTHOR INDEX

SUBJECT INDEX

Note: The letters 'f', 't' and 'b' following the locators refer to figures, tables and boxes respectively.

219